MW00892957

Philippine Birthmark

The Story of William Singleton Carroll

*His birth and first three years
as a prisoner of the Japanese
in the Philippines 1941-45*

Linda — enjoy my friend!

Lean   April 1, 2019

by

McLean Goodpasture Carroll

Philippine Birthmark

The Story of William Singleton Carroll

His birth and first three years
as a prisoner of the Japanese
in the Philippines 1941-45

Contents

Preface

I have known my husband's early story—in part—for nearly 45 years, and I've toyed with the idea of writing something about it for a while. But it was only after deciding to gather my family and actually visit the Philippines that I buckled down.

Research sent me in more directions than I ever thought possible, and the magic of the internet afforded answers that astounded me. Many elements from the stories of other people who endured great privation at the hands of the Japanese have been included, and what amazed me was the corroboration of events from one account to the next. Gathering those pieces of others' experiences gave me enough insight to paint what I hope is a probable picture of the Carroll family's ordeal.

The things I have learned about the War in the Pacific during WWII greatly enhanced the process of writing this story. Although I only touch on a few incidences that relate directly to the narrative, the enormity of the Pacific theater and the sacrifices made by the "Greatest Generation" are astonishing and overwhelming. The fact that Bill and his family survived their capture and imprisonment by the Japanese is really nothing short of a miracle.

This story is for Bill, our children and the extended Carroll family. For the relatives of all the other internees who endured profound suffering and the relatives of those who died while imprisoned, this is also for you.

Note: Throughout the book, I have incorporated parenthesized italics to indicate footnotes. Italics used outside of parentheses denote emphasis.

To

Norwood and Isabel

Philippine Birthmark

The Story of William Singleton Carroll

*His birth and first three years
as a prisoner of the Japanese
in the Philippines 1941-45*

Chapter I

Where to Begin?

"Billy *Carr*oll! Good Lord, son. What's the matter? You're just a wobbly little top spinning out of control! Slow down buddy...what is it?"

"Air-raid, ya dope, air-raid, ya dope!" Moments after Billy's declaration there usually *was* an air raid, and this frantic, somewhat humorous, and seemingly sixth-sense scene, would repeat itself many times in the coming weeks.

The year is 1944. Billy Carroll is almost three years old. He and his father Norwood, mother Isabel, five-year-old brother Lee, and his four-year-old sister Peggy are in Manila, Philippine Islands at the Santo Tomás Internment Camp as special, but reluctant guests of the Imperial Japanese Army. The astonishing and implausible journey here is a harrowing tale.

To begin. Billy's father Norwood Carroll of Warsaw, North Carolina began a career with Liggett & Myers Tobacco Company in 1929, a year after graduating from the University of North Carolina. A die-hard and popular Tar Heel, Norwood played varsity baseball and was elected treasurer of his 1928 Class. In 1931 he was sent from

Durham, North Carolina to the Philippines to serve as the Far Eastern Manager for L&M in Manila.

After three years, Norwood took a brief leave to return home and marry Isabel Singleton of Durham. Isabel, voted one of the prettiest girls in her 1926 high school senior yearbook, was a Duke University alumna. The bitter and storied rivalry between the UNC Tar Heels and the Duke Blue Devils, a rivalry which both she and Norwood embraced and thoroughly enjoyed, didn't seem to matter much to either of them. True love trumped college rivalry.

The happy, handsome couple married and without delay made their way back to Manila via New York, Chicago, and Los Angeles, sailing the final leg of the trip on the passenger ship "President Coolidge." They ended their honeymoon with three more days at the historic and magnificent white, green-tile-roofed Manila Hotel.

Married life in Manila, so very far from home for a 27-year-old bride, began with adventure and a dynamic social life. Norwood, having lived there for three years, naturally had numerous contacts and a wide circle of friends who surely helped ease Isabel into a her new and extraordinarily different lifestyle. Many a rousing weekend evening was spent at the Army and Navy Club with other expats who lived and worked in the city. The club, a beautiful manse situated on a Manila Bay waterfront green, was surrounded by palm and coconut trees and riotously growing bougainvillea. Dinners, soirees and romantic dancing under the stars were the norm. Life was exciting. The parts of the bustling city where the Americans and Europeans lived looked like botanical gardens. Tree-lined boulevards overflowed with pink and blue hydrangeas and fragrant orchids growing unrestrained. Isabel, being a gardener and lover of beautiful flowers, must have been enchanted with her new home.

Eventually, Norwood's job sent him to Panay Island, south of Manila, Luzon, where he and Isabel lived at 221 Jaro, a district in the gulf city of Iloilo. Lee, their first son, was born November 9, 1938 and Peggy, their daughter, followed on December 1, 1939. It was a splendid time, with many domestic servants to lighten the load of childcare and household duties. American women living in the Philippines had cooks, chauffeurs, houseboys, lavenderas, and amahs to care for their children. Rumor has it they were told that cooking and common housework could be *fatal* to a white woman in such a climate, so, generally speaking, it was an easygoing and agreeable existence.

Facts, unfortunately, are few regarding their everyday life, but a few recollections of those days in Iloilo are remembered. Norwood said they had a dog named Spot and a pet monkey. Isabel often regaled friends with the stories of that naughty monkey, the best being the day he got loose in the kitchen and wreaked pure havoc tossing flour, coffee and sugar from opened canisters. While I'm sure there was *little* hyperbole in that story, a monkey loose in the kitchen would certainly be a force to reckon with. Isabel also recalled that when she and the children went down to the harbor to welcome Norwood home from a week "on the road," he, in his white linen suit, would cheerily toss his Panama straw hat to a loyal servant on the dock and stride boldly down the gangplank. Norwood apparently liked tossing his hat. He often recounted how he would enter the bar at their social club, after being away, and fling his hat to the bartender. "If that hat didn't come flying back, I knew it was safe to join the fun." Norwood was quite the wag, and indeed life was good.

For seven years, Norwood and Isabel enjoyed their tropical, storybook life, but then the startling and completely unforeseen happened. The "Army of the Greater Japanese Empire" bombed Pearl Harbor on December 7, 1941, bringing the United States into World War II. On that *same* day—December 8th in the Philippines, east of the International Date Line—ten hours after the sneak attack in

Hawaii, the largest island in the Philippine archipelago, Luzon, was bombed, Camp John Hay at Baguio the first target. Another strike destroyed Fort Stotzenberg, a large defense force intended to protect Luzon, and a third leveled the airfield at Iba. Clark Field, the largest airfield, followed, its obliteration as drastic as Pearl Harbor. Historians have not been kind in chronicling that attack. Apparently, a Filipino telegraph operator was told to report any enemy planes he might see approaching the Philippines. Baguio was bombed within *earshot* of the operator, but because no report came, the pilots at Clark Field left their planes parked wing to wing while they retired to the mess hall to eat their lunch. When Iba was attacked, all radar equipment was destroyed which probably impacted the communication to Clark Field. Nichols Field, south of Manila, was then razed. The entire Philippine air defense was, for practical purposes, completely wiped out. It is hard to imagine the degree of utter surprise. Martin B-10s and Boeing B-17s were the principle planes at the airfields, and only seventeen B-17 bombers and about 40 pursuit planes were left in the arsenals. There were so few airplanes left at Clark Field that the commanding officer commissioned local Chinese craftsmen to build fake planes from wood and canvas to fool the Japanese reconnaissance aircraft.

Before the invasion, many Americans wondered why military defenses were not being reinforced. Talk of war had been stirring in the Philippines for some time because of Japan's forays into China and nearby island nations. Japan's war with China, particularly Manchuria, had been waging since the early 1930s. Massive Japanese ship movements in the South China Sea and troop positions in Indochina made many in Manila insist that war was coming.

One of the Imperial Army's biggest goals was control of the Dutch East Indies, but between Japan and their objective lay a 1,500-mile-long archipelago of 7,107 islands and islets under American command. The Philippines was the only major barrier in Japan's quest to be the master of the Orient.

When people went to the High Commissioner in Manila (*the equivalent to an American Amabassador*) to seek transport to the U.S., they were urged to stay in Manila, then deemed the safest place to be in the Orient. Corregidor, the diminutive tadpole-shaped island in Manila Bay was impenetrable, they were told. General
Douglas MacArthur would never let it fall.

Meanwhile, MacArthur, who had been serving as a military advisor to the Philippine Commonwealth government since 1935, was called out of retirement by

President Roosevelt and named the Commander of the United States Army Forces in the Far East (USAFFE). In his new role, he repeatedly demanded materiél to bolster his defenses. MacArthur believed the Philippine Islands to be of strategic and military importance, but because the American war plans were focused primarily on Europe, it took an inordinate amount of partisan quarreling before the equipment finally began to be appropriated. A few American troop ships arrived in September 1941, increasing the U.S. Army to 31,000 troops (19,000 American and 12,00 Filipino), but by November, a *backlog* of 1,100,000 shipping tons of much needed equipment had accumulated in U.S. ports awaiting vessels. These munitions sitting stateside were of little help to MacArthur in the Philippines. Nevertheless, carrying on, he ordered that defenses be dug into the beaches at the most likely spots of attack on Luzon, while in truth, he believed and insisted that the Japanese would not attack until spring of 1942. A resulting attitude of apathy crept into the newly arriving soldiers. They were enjoying the warm climate, abundant bars and 'ladies of the night'

Many books have disparaged the lack of action on the part of MacArthur. Why did General MacArthur fail to heed the early morning warnings from Pearl Harbor? Why were generals screened and unable to contact him? Was his apparent inaction due to Philippine President Manuel Quezon's desire to remain neutral? Was he waiting for a direct attack? The questions and opinions are as disparate and full of rhetoric as any political or military debate can set forth, so instead of arguing the truth or value of such discourse, the story of the Carroll family will remain the focus.

Norwood and Isabel must have been stunned by the dreadful and staggering news of the attack. Anyone who was not a Filipino citizen feared for their lives. It was only a matter of time before enemy soldiers would invade the other islands south of Luzon. In fact, on December 18, 1941, Iloilo City, about 300 miles south of Manila, suffered its first air raid by 36 bombers. A plan to exit the city was imperative. There was no way to leave the Philippines. Everyone was trapped. But flee the city they must. Taking flight with two young toddlers (Lee was three and Peggy, two) was challenging enough, but Isabel was nine months pregnant with her third child. Besides, *where* would they go?

The newlyweds at Norwood's home in Warsaw,
NC before their voyage to Manila

9

Norwood and Isabel in Waikiki on their way to Manila

A newspaper article referencing the passengers arriving Manila on the "President Coolidge." Norwood and Isabel are top row second from the right

The Manila Hotel

The Army and Navy Club

11

Norwood in front of their home at 221 Jaro in Iloilo City

Norwood on the front steps

Isabel with their dog Spot

Naughty monkey with the cook

Isabel and Norwood with Lee—their first born

Norwood with his Filipino sales group

Chapter II

A Brief Overview of the Philippines' History

Ruled for many years by the Spanish, directly from Madrid under the Crown, the Philippines fell under American dominance after the U.S. defeated Spain in the Spanish-American war of 1898. Puerto Rico, Guam, the Philippines and partial control of Cuba were also ceded to the U.S. at the end of that war. U.S. control of Manila, the capital city, was won through a covert agreement with the Spanish governor-general, Francisco Rizzo. The surrender of Manila was to be secured by waging a mock skirmish. The *Mock Battle of Manila*, not to be confused with the Battle of Manila Bay—the decisive victory in the bay four months earlier by Commodore George Dewey's Asiatic Squadron—ensued on August 13, 1898. The battle is sometimes referred to as the "Mock Battle" because the Spanish and American generals, who were legally still at war, wanted to transfer control of the city center from the Spanish to the Americans while keeping the Philippine Revolutionary Army out. The Spanish were aware of their tenuous position and did not want to lose the war dishonorably, but more important they did not want the

Filipino Revolutionaries to take back control of their country. Such an end would have been more than dishonorable—it would have been unbearable. An agreement was reached. The scheme was for Dewey's force in the bay to lob a few token volleys at the Intramuros, the walled inner city, and the Spanish, after an acceptable interval would then surrender. What should have taken only a few hours with no loss of life ended up being a bloody, all-day battle because of not only badly placed shelling from the bay, but also unexpected Filipino flanking maneuvers south of the city. Nevertheless, that skirmish did ultimately achieve its goal, and the American forces gained control of the Intramuros. The following day, August 14th, the terms of the Spanish capitulation were signed, and the American governance of the Philippines began.

Later in the year, in December, after the Americans were victorious and firmly in control of the Intramuros, the Treaty of Paris was signed ending the war with Spain, and the Philippine Islands were sold to the United States for $20 million. It was with this treaty that Spanish rule formally ended.

A remarkable and perhaps marginally known detail of this war was that General Arthur MacArthur, Jr, Douglas MacArthur's father, was sent to the Philippines in August of

1898 by President William McKinley to spearhead an eleven-thousand-man expeditionary force under the command of Major General Wesley Merritt. These men were part of the ground forces, along with Filipino allies that set up the maneuvers for Dewey's mock battle attack, and under MacArthur's command they fought valiantly.

It was Major General Merritt, in accordance with instructions from President McKinley after the Treaty of Paris was signed, who issued a proclamation announcing the establishment of the U.S. military rule. On May 5, 1900, Merritt named General Arthur MacArthur, Jr. the provost marshal general and military governor of Manila. Douglas MacArthur's older brother, Naval Ensign Arthur III, received news of the appointment while on a warship off Luzon while young Douglas was home preparing to enter West Point. Arthur MacArthur served in that capacity until July 4, 1901. Consequently the Philippines and the name MacArthur have a remarkably historical and familial connection.

The Philippine Revolutionary forces which were once former allies of the United States, were furious that they were now under U.S. control. Still surrounding the Intramuros, the Revolutionary forces objected to the treaty terms and consequently created the conditions for the

Second Battle of Manila five months later on February 4, 1899. The Philippine-American War, also called the Philippine Insurrection raged on for three more years. It took 150,000 "goddamns" to defeat the "gugus" (*The names the GIs gave themselves and the natives*), with the revolution officially ending on July 2, 1902 in victory for the United States. Some Filipino guerilla groups, though, continued to battle the American forces for several more years, mostly on Mindanao 500 miles to the south. The insurgents killed tens of thousands, and the nation was split in polemic debate, not unlike Vietnam

The war and occupation by the U.S. changed the cultural landscape of the islands as the citizens dealt with an estimated 200,000 to 250,000 total Filipino civilians dead. The Catholic Church dissolved as the state religion of the islands. The English language was introduced as the primary language of government, education, business, industry, and increasingly among families and educated individuals. Many of the American soldiers brought to this unknown land decided to stay after the war, hoping to find fortune in a new frontier, and many of them, indeed, did prosper.

Nearly fifty years of U.S. occupation brought modernity and affluence to the islands. Agricultural reform, education, infrastructure, public health—these were just part of what American colonialism afforded. Manila became known as the Pearl of the Orient with modern-day conveniences alongside the old Spanish culture. During this time over 7,000 Americans were born in the Philippines, it being the only home they had ever known. Filipinos became more Americanized than they realized. They seemed to be fine with foreign cultures as long as they were not dominated by them. Love for the Americans grew, and Commonwealth status was eventually granted in 1934 through the Philippine Independence Act. This act allowed for a limited form of independence and established a process for ending U.S. autonomy. Originally scheduled for 1944, Philippine sovereignty was delayed by World War II, but finally, through the Treaty of Manila, signed on July 4, 1946, (an auspicious date) independence was granted.

American and European enterprise flourished in the Philippines. The islands were rich in natural resources—gold, oil and lumber to name a few. U.S. companies like American Express, Otis Elevator, Goodyear Tire and Rubber, West Coast Life Insurance Company, International Harvester Company, American Chamber of Commerce, the Rockefeller Foundation, and Liggett & Myers Tobacco Company were some of the many companies launched during the 1930s. With the establishment of the islands as a source of raw materials and a market for European manufacturers, much local wealth was created with the Filipinos also prospering. The average Filipino benefited from the new economy because of the increased demand for labor as well as the opportunities for business enterprise. Early decades of the 20th Century were good times for many living in Manila and its environs, and it was during these years that Norwood and Isabel made the Philippines their home. One might say that they were living the life of Riley.

The Battle of Manila Bay

General Arthur MacArthur, Jr.
Douglas MacArthur's father

Chapter III

The Flight to the Jungle

As the Japanese closed in, time was running out for the Carrolls to leave Iloilo City. Safeguarding personal treasures and planning a safe route for the trip was an enormous responsibility for Norwood. With a wife, two small children and a baby due any day, it had to be overwhelming for him. Several loyal Filipino servants vowed to shelter, as best they could, much of the valuable rugs and furniture. Jewelry was stored in cans and buried in the yard. Foodstuffs, clothing, bedding, medicines all had to be packed and transported, but how and where?

Several years ago, a treasure trove of elementary and high school pictures of Bill was sent to him from his brother Lee. Bill had no idea why Lee had all those pictures or what he was supposed to do with them, but in that box was a moldy, mildewed little book that no one had ever mentioned before. This little book was Bill's baby book written in the hand of his mother, Isabel, in 1942. The information therein paints the perfect picture of the family's journey. Let it tell the story.

Inscribed on inside page:

Lee Singleton Carroll (*Lee is actually Norwood Lee*)
From his loving grandmother Carroll
Wishing him a long and useful life Xmas 1938

Jan. 28, 1942

This book, not having been used for Lee, is being brought into use for Billy (William Singleton Carroll).

Billy is one-month old today. He was born on December 28, 1941 in Janiuay, Philippine Islands. He weighed between 8 ½ and 9 pounds at birth. He was born in the house we occupied in the little town.

On December 7, the Japanese bombed Pearl Harbor and attacked the Philippine Islands. From there on, our lives were lived in fear and anxiety. The Japanese bombed our town, Iloilo, about two weeks later. We had fortunately just finished an air raid shelter in our yard, to which we fled to safety. The town was pretty badly wrecked. Billy being due in a short time, we decided it best to leave Iloilo for a safer place, so several families of us took a house up over a school house in Janiuay. The men drove from Iloilo every day or two to see us and bring supplies. (*This distance is about 28 miles, which on today's road takes about one hour and ten minutes to travel. There were five families altogether.*)

Iloilo was bombed again five days after the first attack. We left Iloilo Christmas Eve. Christmas was a pretty grim affair, but our husbands were with us and we were safe, so we were thankful. All women and children were evacuated from Iloilo and the Army was preparing for an invasion. Billy arrived at 8:40 a.m. (*Only three days after reaching Janiuay!*) Dr. Waters had arrived the night before, after we sent a message to come. We rigged up the top of a clothes basket as a bed for him.

We were afraid of being on the main road where fighting would take place in case of invasion, so the men found a place in the hills to bring us. On the tenth day of Billy's life we started our trek. An Army officer friend borrowed an Army command car to move me as I couldn't stand the truck ride. After an hour's ride over a bumpy road and having crossed rivers fourteen times, we arrive at a Chinese house where we had previously sent our provisions. (*There is no mention of where this house was located.*) There, we found carabao sleds to bring us here. Our mattresses, stores, etc. were piled on these, as well as the people, and we began to walk through wild country. (*These sleds were pulled by carabaos, a swamp-type water buffalo.*)

I was carried in a hammock and the baby in another. After an hour's tramp, we arrived at a little school house where we spent the night. There was only one room and the twelve of us slept in it. Also, we had tins of kerosene and all our cases of tinned goods in it. It was very difficult getting the children fed, as well as ourselves, and bedded down for the night.

The next morning, we started out again for our destination. We arrived, some hiking, some on carabao sleds, and the baby and I in our hammocks, here in a little valley in the hills. There was at the time our nipa (palm) house, which consisted of one room, half a floor, and a ground underneath full of pigs and roosters. The workmen were frantically trying to finish the bamboo floor with about twelve people all over the place and Lee and Peggy falling through the floor and having to be rescued each second.

The baby's bed was set up, and mine, so we could rest, and then the unloading of the sleds began. It was really a nightmare. One couldn't walk for the luggage, tinned goods, bedding etc. in the middle of the floor. Starting stoves, chow, feeding the baby every three hours, day and night, was certainly no picnic. Next day we started moving the stuff back against the walls and got the floor finished.

Each night there were about fifteen of us sleeping in one room, the servants also. There were no toilet facilities and the water had to be brought from a spring. When one got up at night, all that he could see was a mass of mosquito nets over bedding put down on the floor. If you walked across the floor, there was the danger of stepping in someone's face and having your neck cut off by a string holding someone's net up. And on top of that, Billy cried at night so much that nobody could sleep. We lost all modesty by having to dress and undress in one room, but that is a small matter. We are in a quiet place where we don't hear the rumble of army trucks all day and night going by the house carrying troops and supplies. We don't have the fear of planes bombing us, as we did before we came here, although we can't feel altogether safe as long as there is fear of invasion.

We have been here about twenty days now and have made rapid progress. Our house, a nipa one with two rooms, was completed first. The three children and two amahs sleep in one, and Carroll and I in the other. (*Carroll was Isabel's moniker for Norwood.*) Since we moved in, there have been three other houses completed and part of another. The families are gradually getting out of the original house and into their own. All of us eat at the original house, where the cooking is done. I have a kerosene burner in our house and we feed the children here. Today, at one month, Billy weighs 10½ pounds, which is remarkable considering what he has been through. I failed to state in this narrative that his shade over the hammock on our trek up here, was a banana leaf held over him by the amah, as she walked by his hammock.

February 11

Weighed Billy today and he tipped the scales at exactly twelve pounds, nice going for a six weeks old babe. He looks grand and smiles at us.

There is not much to relate since my last notation. We heard that one of our friends who had been put in a concentration camp in Manila had committed suicide. Our other friends up there are probably very hungry. It doesn't make us feel any too good.

Sunday, we had several visitors in our compound. Three Army officers, formerly friends in Iloilo, came in and had chow with us. Visitors always pep us up

All the houses are finished, and the families are settled. There are five small houses and the big house. There are six families in all, three British and three American. It seems incredible to think that all of us slept in one room for such a long time.

We have plowed the field in the middle of our compound and have set out our garden. There are several different kinds of vegetables. The flower seeds have also been set out. If we could have a nice rain now, everything would be fine.

April 1

Billy became ill about two weeks ago with gastro-enteritis. I was scared to death that it was dysentery. Carroll went to the hospital in Calinog (*This town is 18 miles from Januiay, so a triangulation with these two towns and their trek on foot gives a hint as to the location of their hide-away.*) and sent medicine and instructions from Dr. Waters the next day. He seems to be all right now. He lost weight from being taken off milk but is gaining it back. He weighs thirteen pounds now and laughs out loud and follows us with his eyes.

We have been getting lettuce from our garden for about three weeks now and the beets and other vegetables are coming along nicely. We have just finished building air raid shelters back of each house. Dug right in the hill, in case of dog fights by the airplanes, we shall need them. Every time we hear a plane, the women get frightened.

Peggy and Lee are in the sun all day, and they are brown as Indians. They are well and seem happy. They are so difficult tho'. They almost drive me nuts at times.

This is the last entry by Isabel. Since it is known that they were eventually captured by the Japanese, one can perhaps assume that it was soon after this last notation their hideout was discovered. It was actually nearly two months later. While doing research I fortuitously came across A.V.H Hartendorp's book *The Japanese Occupation of the Philippines*. The following summarized account answers many of the questions regarding what happened to the Carrolls after their capture that were never before communicated.

A company of ten men and women and five children, of whom one was a baby only a few weeks old, had established a camp hidden in the hills near the sitio of Cunsad, 8 kilometers from the highway at a point some 25 kilometers from the town of Passi. Here the Carrolls, the McCrearys, the Greenbaums, the Churchills, and the Davises built five shacks and live unmolested for several months after the Japanese had occupied the island. But on **June 23, 1942,** around 3 o'clock in the afternoon, a Japanese lieutenant and seven soldiers,

31

guided by a renegade Filipino, surprised the camp. Armed with rifles and a machine gun, they were suddenly seen spread out fanwise and closing in on the little colony. There was no chance for anyone to escape.

The first thing the Japanese did was to search the shacks for firearms, but the people had none. (*Hartendorp's account mentions nothing about putting everyone in a firing line. Norwood recounts that as he stood with Lee and Peggy–Isabel with Billy in her arms–his eye was trained on the Lieutenant's trigger finger. He surely must have been thankful that no guns were purchased from their Army friends, when offered earlier, because when no arms were found, the finger released. Isabel often said she felt they were spared because the Japanese like children. However, a group of missionaries, the Hopevale Martyrs, hiding a bit north, were captured sometime after, and every single soul was killed–adults beheaded, and children bayoneted.*)

The Japanese lieutenant and his men were courteous enough with the people when they found them to be civilians and unarmed, but they appropriated all the tooth paste in sight and some loose money, and they took three of the men and a 15-year-old boy with them, telling one man, N.M. Carroll, who was suffering from a tropical ulcer on his leg, and the women and children, to remain where they were. A bus was waiting for the soldiers and their four prisoners at the road (*There is no indication of the distance from the hideaway to this road or what road it was unless this was the highway indicated earlier as 8 kilometers distant from their lair.*) and they reached Passi at 10 o'clock that night. They slept at a private house which had been converted into Japanese headquarters, in the same room with their captors, and were taken to the local convent the next day, where they were very kindly treated by the Filipino padre.

The following day, the 25th, one of the men, G. H. W. Churchill (manager of the Asiatic Petroleum Company branch at Iloilo), was taken back to Cunsad under the same escort plus a Japanese captain, arriving about noon. His wife and all the others had been greatly worried about the fate of the four and were very happy to see Churchill. They were now told they would all have to come to Passi and the Japanese officers insisted that they take along everything they had there, not only in the way of supplies but every article of use. It was all hauled down the trail on some 30 carabao sleds. The few farmers in the neighborhood and their sons were pressed into service, and it was quite a safari that finally started to move toward the road. As it had to cross the small Swagi river (*Suage*) many times, everything got wet. Carroll was at first carried in a hammock, but after a few kilometers the soldiers forced him to walk and put the mother with the small baby and two other children into the hammock. Carroll struggled along on his own sore leg, Churchill, however, carrying him across the river each time on his back. (*It was amazing to learn this never told story from Hartendorp's book.*)

At the road, several automobiles and trucks for the baggage were waiting for the party. One of the trucks had to be towed. The tow-rope was short, and the brake was defective, a driving rain set in, and it was dark before the party reached Passi. The baggage was left at headquarters except for the bedding and some handbags, and the people were taken to the convent. The Japanese said that there would be "inspections" during the night, and the possible implications of this so frightened everybody that one of the husbands set up his cot in front of the door of the women's room, not putting up his mosquito net in order to keep himself awake. Twice that night a patrol marched up to the convent and tramped through the sleeping quarters, flashing on their electric torches inquisitively. Nothing else happened but the same performance was repeated nightly as long as they stayed there.

The next morning, they were allowed to take only some food for the children from all their supplies. A Japanese explained to them that a General had passed through and had given orders that the soldiers should take everything they needed from the supplies belonging to the party, as "the Army came first". Japanese soldiers gave them some cigarettes and also small quantities of tea. Apart from this, the Japanese took practically everything that they had, not only the comestibles but their clothing, too.

They spent five nights at the convent and were then taken by train to Pototan. The train was waiting on the other side of the Passi bridge, which had been partly blown up by the USAFFE, (*The United States Army Force of the Far East, was commanded first by Douglas MacArthur and later General Jonathan Wainwright),* and the whole group had to cross this long, high bridge on foot, on the ties and some planks placed across the gaps, a dizzy and dangerous performance, especially for the women and children. They had started late and did not reach Pototan, where the train stopped, until after dark. The Japanese wanted them to spend the night in the unlighted, 3rd-class carriage they were riding in, but the people protested that they had to have food for the children and they were then permitted to spend the night in the nearby house of a kind

34

Filipino family, the Magbanuas, where they were given an excellent meal and made as comfortable as possible. About 9 o'clock the next morning they were again herded aboard the train for Iloilo, 35 kilometers farther down the line. Before they left, Mrs. Magbanua played some old songs for them on her piano, including "Auld Lang Syne" and "Home Sweet Home", which brought tears to the eyes of the women, worn out by their experiences of the past week and fearful of what might still face them.

The party had been accompanied from Passi by only one Japanese soldier-guard and when they reached the Iloilo station, there was only one Japanese soldier there to meet them. In fact, he was the only man visible in the whole station. They then walked to the school house on the Molo road, about a kilometer away, and again they had to cross a bridge, the Forbes Bridge, with its blown-up span. The Iloilo camp looked like a heavenly refuge to the weary people from Cunsad, who had not known what terrors might still be in store for them. The women fell into the arms of their friends in the camp and again there were a few tears, this time of relief.

Since the Japanese soldiers took everything from their captives—money, toothpaste, bedding—it begs the question of how did Isabel safeguard little Billy's babybook? Did she hide it in her undergarments? All the packed clothing was thoroughly searched. But regardless of the method, her forethought protected a most precious piece of history that remained untouched for the better part of sixty-five years.

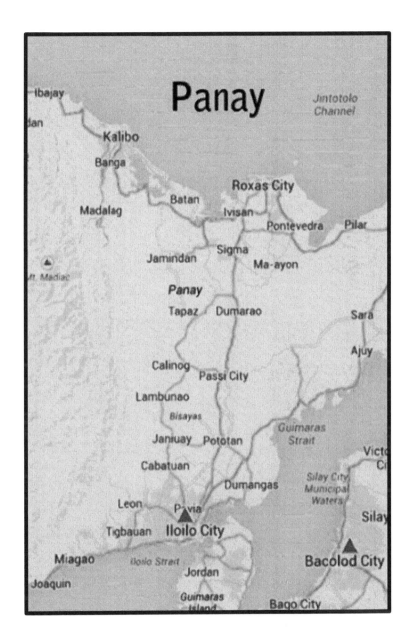

Iloilo City and the roads to Janiuay, Pototan and Passi City

Jungle pictures

The Suage River

Passi City

Passi Bridge

The convent in Passi City where the group spent five nights

TERESA MAGBANUA
October 13, 1868 - August, 1947

Teresa Magbanua y Ferraris (October 13, 1868 — August 1947) earned the distinction of being the only woman to lead combat troops in the Visayas against Spanish and American forces. Born in Pototan, Iloilo, Philippines on 13 October 1868, to wealthy parents, she earned a teaching degree and taught in her hometown. Having come from a family of revolutionaries, she immediately volunteered her services to the motherland and became an exceptional horseman and marksman. Fifty years later, her heroism was once again displayed when she helped finance a guerrilla resistance movement by the liberators together with the Allied Filipino soldiers of the 6th, 61st and 62nd Infantry Division of the Philippine Commonwealth Army, 6th Infantry Regiment of the Philippine Constabulary and the Ilonggo guerrillas against the Japanese in the Battle for the Liberation of Iloilo. Teresa Magbanua was likely called the "Joan of Arc" of the Philippines.

Carabao—Filipino water buffalo

Carabao sled

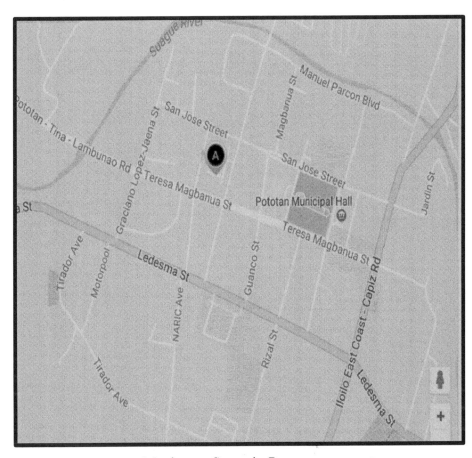

Magbanua Street in Pototan

Chapter IV

The Invasion. What was happening?

While the Carrolls and the other families were hiding in the jungle, the Japanese were swiftly gaining full control of the islands. After the bombing of the airbases on Luzon and attacks on Naval ships at Cavite, 130,000 American and Filipino troops, many ill-trained and untried, were met by 43,000 hardened enemy Japanese at Lingayen Gulf 126 miles northwest of Manila on December 21st. In relatively short order, despite having a three-to-one advantage over the aggressor, the U.S. Army was overrun and forced to retreat to Bataan, a thumb shaped peninsula between Manila and the South China Sea. With the astonishingly rapid advance of the Japanese troops, General MacArthur decided to transfer his headquarters of the USAFFE to the island stronghold of Corregidor at the entrance of Manila Bay. On December 26th he declared Manila an Open City. It was his hope to save the Pearl of the Orient from complete destruction, but with his retreat, the city was abandoned, and its civilians left defenseless. MacArthur and his family stayed in Malinta Tunnel where huge quantities of ammunition, food, essential supplies and a 1,000-bed hospital were set up underground (*The tunnel, an 835-foot-long and 24-foot-wide excavation with several laterals, was dug into a 390-foot ridge by the U.S. Army Corps of Engineers in 1932 after World War I to rectify the lack of fortifications and defenses on the island.).*

All crucial food supplies for the soldiers had earlier been entrenched on the beachheads near the gulf awaiting an assault that MacArthur believed would not happen until the spring of 1942, so *no* provisions were available on Bataan. This was a grave and terribly unfortunate miscalculation.

With such a swift and potent assault by the Japanese, Washington, understandably, did not want a general of MacArthur's prominence to be captured. So upon orders from President Roosevelt, MacArthur, with his family and several staff officers, left Corregidor on March 12th for Mindanao. Command of the USAFFE was given to General Jonathan Wainwright with a name change to United States Forces in the Philippines (USFIP). Before his departure, MacArthur made Wainwright promise that throughout his command it be made clear that his leaving was under repeated protests. "If I get through to Australia, you know I will come back as soon as I can and with as much as I can."

MacArthur prepared to leave, and as he walked to the dock he shook the hand of every man who came to see him off. Tears overtook some as they realized this was the end for them. One asked his sergeant what MacArthur's chances were of reaching Australia. The answer: maybe one in five.

After a hair-raising 35-hour journey on four PT boats—braving mines, rough seas, and the Japanese navy— MacArthur told his boat's commander, John D. Bulkeley, "You've taken me out of the jaws of death, and I won't forget it." Shortly after reaching Mindanao, MacArthur flew to Australia where he was given command of all the Allied forces in the Southwest Pacific. Upon arrival there, MacArthur found far fewer Allied troops in Australia than he had hoped for to relieve his trapped forces on Bataan. Deeply disappointed, it was then he famously vowed to his men and the Filipino people, "I shall return!"

For 99 days the combined troops on Bataan, crippled by starvation and disease, with no naval or air support bravely resisted the Imperial Army until April 9, 1942, when they were forced to surrender. More than 76,000 starving and emaciated American and Filipino soldiers, now under the command of General Edward King, laid down their arms (*Wainwright had ceded his command for Bataan to General King while he positioned the remaining troops on Corregidor.*). It was the single largest defeat in American military history. MacArthur's promises to the weary soldiers before he left Corregidor that relief ships and planes were coming were fallacious. The Philippines were cut off, thanks to the obliteration of Pearl Harbor, and the Japanese had control of the waters from the Bering Strait to the Coral Sea. There was no hope for rescue. Washington knew it (*The focus of the war was on Europe.*) and so, now, did MacArthur. Those brave souls, the "Battling Bastards of Bataan," were sitting ducks. In derision they called MacArthur "Dugout Doug" and sang a ditty to the tune of "The Battle Hymn of the Republic."

> Dugout Doug MacArthur lies a shaking on the Rock,
> Safe from all the bombers and from any sudden shock.
> Dougout Doug is eating of the best food on Bataan
> And his troops go starving on.

Why did MacArthur give false hope to those embattled troops? It is hard to comprehend. Some will say a leader must inspire and motivate even when he knows the chips are down.

The following is a radio broadcast from the Voice of Freedom transmitted from Malinta Tunnel on April 9, 1942.

Bataan has fallen. The Philippine-American troops on this war-ravaged and bloodstained peninsula have laid down their arms. With heads bloody but unbowed, they have yielded to the superior force and numbers of the enemy.

The world will long remember the epic struggle that Filipino and American soldiers put up in the jungle fastness and along the rugged coast of Bataan. They have stood up uncomplaining under the constant and grueling fire of the enemy for more than three months. Besieged on land and blockaded by sea, cut off from all sources of help in the Philippines and in America, the intrepid fighters have done all that human endurance could bear.

For what sustained them through all these months of incessant battle was a force that was more than merely physical. It was the force of an unconquerable faith— something in the heart and soul that physical hardship and adversity could not destroy. It was the thought of native land and all that it holds most dear, the thought of freedom and dignity and pride in these most priceless of all our human prerogatives.

The adversary, in the pride of his power and triumph, will credit our troops with nothing less than the courage and fortitude that his own troops have shown in battle. Our men have fought a brave and bitterly contested struggle. All the world will testify to the most superhuman endurance with which they stood up until the last in the face of overwhelming odds.

But the decision had to come. Men fighting under the banner of unshakable faith are made of something more than flesh, but they are not made of impervious steel. The flesh must yield at last, endurance melts away, and the end of the battle must come.

Bataan has fallen, but the spirit that made it stand—a beacon to all the liberty-loving peoples of the world—cannot fall

What followed that defeat, the Bataan Death March, was one of the most horrific forced marches ever recorded. 80,000 American and Filipino soldiers, with no food or water, staggered in searing heat to a railhead in San Fernando more than *sixty-five miles* away. If they stumbled or fell, they were shot. If they tried to get water, they were shot. The Japanese shot, beheaded, or bayoneted so many starving men that they left a dead body every fifteen yards. Once they reached the railhead, the soldiers were crammed—standing room only—into small unsanitary boxcars to travel farther north to Capas. Upright and unable to move, many soldiers died standing in excrement and vomit. Their five-day misery ended with an additional march for seven miles to Camp O'Donnell, a former Philippine training center. Cruel physical abuse and ruthless slaughter saw thousands die—5,000 to 18,000 Filipino (reports differ widely) and 5,000 to 6,500 American soldiers. Incredibly, 10,000 to 12,000 bold men escaped to the mountains and joined guerilla groups, successfully tying down Japanese efforts going forward.

The Japanese were wholly unprepared for such an enormous number of prisoners in their care. The root of the brutality heaped on these men lay in the Japanese attitude toward a soldier who surrenders—a soldier should die before laying down his arms. A warrior's surrender meant the forfeiture of all rights to treatment as a human being. The Japanese held back nothing in their savage brutality toward these starved and diseased soldiers.

After the victory on Bataan, units of the Japanese 14th Army moved on to Corregidor. General Wainwright had earlier moved over 12,000 troops from Bataan to Corregidor to defend it as the remaining last Allied stronghold. The island, though, was also cut off from reinforcements and supplies from the U.S., and while they managed to sink many Japanese barges as they approached the northern shores, the Allied troops, after weeks of relentless artillery fire, could no longer hold off the invader. The determined and tenacious foe landed dogged troops and boundary shredding tanks. Throughout the conflict, Wainwright was often engaged directly in battle, jumping from foxhole to foxhole, encouraging his men, firing his hand-gun at the advancing enemy, and deservedly earning the nickname "The Last Fighting General."

But the foe was too strong, and to avoid a complete massacre, having already lost 800 men, Wainwright was forced to yield on May 6, 1942. His offer to Japanese General Masaharu Homma was to surrender Corregidor, but Homma wanted the complete, unconditional capitulation of all American forces throughout the Philippines. Wainwright had little choice given the odds against him and the poor physical condition of his troops. He surrendered at midnight, and all 11,200 surviving Allied troops were evacuated to a prison stockade in Manila.

General MacArthur did not want such a complete surrender. He wanted the troops further south in Mindanao to disperse as guerillas with the Filipinos, but Wainwright encouraged all to surrender to General Homma. Wainwright spent over two years as the highest-ranking POW of that conflict, believing he was an utter failure. Justifiably, even after MacArthur vetoed the distinction due to the dishonor of surrender, Wainwright received the Medal of Honor from President Truman after the war.

Did the Carrolls and their fellow prisoners have any knowledge of these battles and surrenders while hiding in the jungle? One would probably think not, but as earlier cited in Isabel's diary, they had army officer friends come visit from time to time. In fact, a USAFFE major told them that one morning before the unconditional surrender ordered by Wainwright, his men had refused to assemble. They announced they were deserting. Even though it was admittedly unsoldierly, the soldiers said it was better to be free in the jungle than to rot in a Japanese prisoner camp. Whether they were more successful evading capture than the Carrolls' group is unknown.

So, yes, it is entirely possible that news of the war effort made it to their lair from time to time, even if nothing is mentioned in the diary

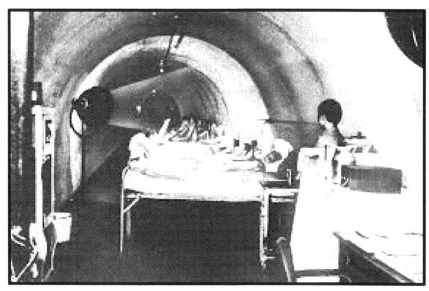

Hospital in Malinta Tunnel

The Bataan Death March

The Death March

The American reaction to the Death March back home

General King with Major General Kameichiro Nagano to surrender
his Bataan forces.

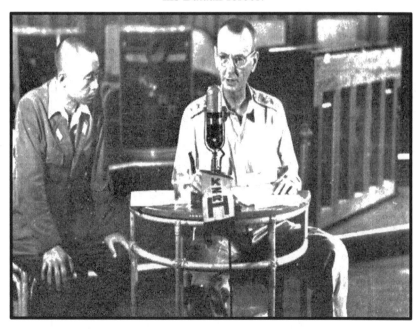

General Masaharu Homma and General Wainwright at the
surrender of all U.S. Forces

58

The troops exiting the Malinta Tunnel on Corregidor

Chapter V

Life in Iloilo City Internment Camp

After their capture and weary journey, the Carrolls are now back in Iloilo City, and on July 4, 1942 they were interned in the Iloilo Central school house where they remained for one year. The school, on the corner of General Luna and Mabini streets, was a five-room concrete building sited on a yard measuring about 150 by 300 feet. Norwood always remarked how July 4th is a day of celebration for Americans, but for him and his family, it was the day of imprisonment. The Iloilo City Internment Camp population had reached 100 prisoners by June of 1942. With the arrival of the Carrolls and the other families, the population was now 115. Their imprisoned daily existence is further summarized from Hartendorp's book, most of that which is recorded taking place prior to the Carrolls' arrival.

In the school yard, there was a small domestic science building where the internees found dishes and cutlery. One room of this building was occupied by the two civilian Japanese guards who were the only Japanese on the premises, but there were barracks across the street and the streets around the school house guarded by Japanese sentries. The internees erected a small cook-house and a number of shower-rooms and toilets in the yard and also dug two wells for water for washing and bathing purposes. Drinking water was obtained from the St. Augustine Convent nearby. (*This was allowed only after large drums of water brought into the camp with holes in the bottom couldn't be fixed by the internees when told to do so. They had nothing with which to solder the holes.*) The Japanese required the internees to build a fence of galvanized-iron sheets set upright all around the school ground and when they noticed that the internees, sitting on the verandah, could still look over this fence, it was raised another eight feet. They also made their own wooden beds, tables, benches, and folding chairs, and even some pots and pans from galvanized-iron sheets.

On May 27, the internees were told that they had been transferred to the control of the Japanese "civil administration", but they could not see that this made any difference. On May 30, they elected Dr. H. Waters, a physician, as their chairman (*This is the same doctor who delivered little Billy–he had been captured earlier, not having fled to the jungle.*). All this time, the internees had to provision themselves, living on what supplies they had been able to take with them or could buy with their own money.

This was the most unbelievable and difficult aspect of their internment. The Japanese did not provide food or bedding! For the greater part of their incarceration, the internees had to live on money that they already had or that loaned by friends. Some or maybe all of Norwood's money was taken when captured in the jungle. Those captured, who had no friends or servants, had to rely on the largesse of other internees or Filipinos in the town. The Filipino and Spanish friends proved their friendship and staunch loyalty over and again, often at significant risk to themselves. It is not known if friends or former servants of the Carrolls brought them food or money, but since they had lived in Iloilo City for several years it was surely possible that they did.

The Japanese asked the internees to pass a resolution "authorizing" the Japanese to sell their household goods and other personal possessions, the proceeds of which would be used for their subsistence. Of course, they had no choice in passing such a resolution, but nothing to their knowledge was ever realized. It was already common knowledge that their homes and offices had been stripped bare, and the Japanese *said* that their goods were warehoused in a local storage unit. Nothing was ever discussed years later about the Carrolls' household goods suffering that end as Norwood always said his servants safeguarded them, and it was his prior preparations for fleeing the city that probably saved many of their treasures from being taken by the Japanese.

Daily life was dull. Roll call was established each morning and lights were out by 9:30 at night. Work was carried out by the able-bodied, and early on no disciplinary problems arose. Drinking problems were nil as there was no alcohol, but booze did make its way into camp on occasion, and several men, of course, over-imbibed. Rules for abstention had to be decided upon and enforced, both by the Japanese and the internees. Catholic masses and Protestant services were allowed, and classes were held for the children in the usual school subjects. Every effort was made by the internees to make life as normal as possible.

Entertainment, basic but essential to the everyone's well-being, was attempted with occasional musicals and dramatic performances. At first, the camp had only one accordion, but a priest soon brought in a small reed organ to augment the musical inventory, and behold, this led to the organization of a choir. To revisit Hartendorp's account:

It was decided to sing the "Hallelujah Chorus" on Easter, and the necessary rehearsals were begun. On such confined premises, these became somewhat obtrusive, and long after Easter the internees still heard ringing in their ears, "Hall-le-lu-jah! Hallelujah-hallelujah, Hal-le-LUHU-jah!" Toward the end of the internment in Iloilo, a phonograph was brought in, but there were only three records; after a few days these were firmly put away.

One year was spent by the Carrolls in the Iloilo City Internment Camp. Life was not terribly horrific—they had shelter and food—but it had to be frustrating to have no control of daily life. Bowing and scraping to an enemy jailer

64

had to be infruriating. On June 16, 1943, with only two hours' notice, the internees were told to pack up their meager belongings and prepare to leave the camp. No opportunity to communicate with local friends was given before they were trucked to the wharf to board the M.S. *Alabat* and be "accommodated" on deck. Only those who were brought from the hospital stayed in a cabin. It is hard to imagine what must have been going through Norwood and Isabel's minds, getting on that ship with the three small children—all under the age of five— knowing only that they would be interned someplace new. The ship went east to Bacolod, Negros and remained at that pier until the morning of the 20th *(This is four days waiting on the ship.)*, unloading rice, sugar, a car and taking on alcohol, salted hides and 15 Japanese soldiers. From Bacolod, the *Alabat* followed a round-about course to Manila, making it a 500 instead of 300-mile voyage skirting the coast of Panay and the east coast of Masbate before crossing over to follow the west coast of Luzon.

After *seven* days' voyage, the ship reached Manila at 10 o'clock in the morning. When the *Alabat* docked at the pier, the passengers were held on board till late in the afternoon, a muggy and uncomfortable interlude. One can only imagine the behavior of three tired and hot young children.

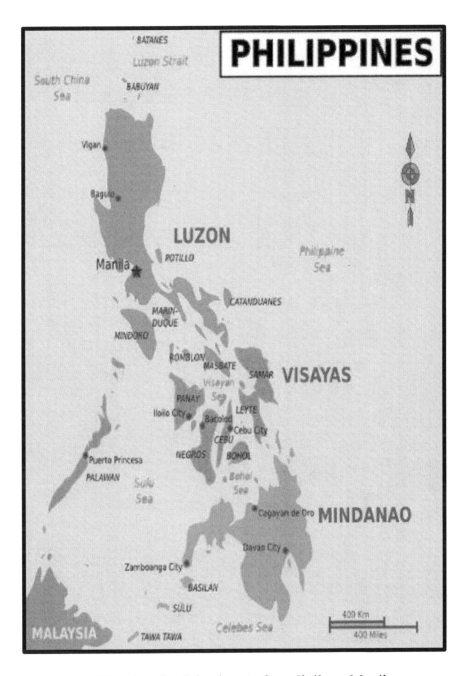

Map showing island route from Iloilo to Manila

AMERICAN CIVILIANS INTERNED IN THE
ILOILO CITY INTERNMENT CAMP PHILIPPINE ISLANDS

NO.	OCCUPATION		NAME		AGE
1	None		E.F.	BOWMAN	48
2	Farmer		FRANKWORTH	BROWN	60
3	Missionary (Mr. 7. Cassanave)		R.C.	BUCHNER	40
4	Employee		H.P.	BYRD	33
5	Priest		HENRY	CARR	34
6	Salesman		N.M.	CARROLL	35
7	None	Mrs.	ISABEL	CARROLL	34
8	None		N.L.	CARROLL	3-1/2
9	None	Miss	M.M.	CARROLL	2-1/2
10	None		W.S.	CARROLL	8 months
11	Employee		EMILIO	CASSANAVE	56
12	Photographer		PEDRO	CASSANAVE	32
13	Employee		THEODORE	CASSANAVE	46
14	Priest		J.V.	CASEY	30
15	Missionary		R.F.	CHAMBERS	40
16	" (Mrs. R.F.)	Mrs.	D.J.	CHAMBERS	40
17	None	Miss	C.J.	CHAMBERS	4
18	"		R.B.	CHAMBERS	2
19	Mining Engineer		A.C.	DAKIN	51
20	None	Mrs.	M.B.	DAKIN	41
21	"	Miss	ALICE	EMERSON	9 months
22	Farmer		AUSE	EMERSON	65

Listing of American civilians at Iloilo City Internment Camp

The Alabat which transported the Carrolls to Manila

CHAPTER VI

Santo Tomás Internment Camp
STIC

It is now June 23, 1943, and Billy is one and a half years old. The Carrolls, along with all the other passengers, were transported off the ship's deck, loaded onto buses and trucks, driven about three miles through the eerily deserted streets of Manila and summarily deposited on the campus of Santo Tomás University, an established internment camp of nearly 4,000 non-combatants. This was a surprise to everyone on the ship as they had been told they were going to Los Baños, an internment camp established north of Manila to house the overflow from STIC. Their arrival was also a surprise to the STIC internees. There had been rumors that the ship was lost at sea. Walking through the iron gate of that university must have been a grim and demoralizing affair. The enormity of that camp compared to Iloilo was surely dizzying, and registering the new internees was a long and miserable process. "It was a bitter day when they registered us at Santo Tomás Prison and the gates closed in on us," said Norwood. "For the sake of the children, we prayed that captivity at least might bring food for them."

STIC was not a prison, as stated by Norwood, per se. It was technically an internment camp that the Japanese, in December 1941, established on the grounds of the Royal and Pontifical University of Santo Tomás, a Spanish Dominican institution founded in 1611. But semantics aside— internment camp, concentration camp—it was their prison.

The walled compound with its spacious grounds— around 65 acres—was chosen by the Japanese in 1941 in agreement with the High Commissioner Francis Sayer and the Red Cross as the most suitable site to house the substantial Manila population. The Main Building, a massive Spanish-style structure of gray stone, with a high-arched doorway and domed tower dominated the open courtyard. The Education Building, a smaller three-story structure, a gymnasium with a great arched roof, a wooden annex, a wooden dormitory and the larger Seminary Building completed the university grounds. Inside the Main Building, from the main floor to the mezzanine, the walls were covered with large oil paintings in ornate frames, most of them gifts from Spanish royalty and the Papacy, depicting the Virgin Mary and the life of Jesus and various saints. These ancient Catholic art treasures framed a massive maze of confused, frightened people and their possessions—a hideous irony.

On Christmas Day 1941, soon after the Japanese entered Manila, a published newspaper statement from the High Commissioner and President Manuel L. Quezon informed the Manilans that at the request of General MacArthur they were also leaving the city for the safety of the government. The Japanese unsurprisingly refused to completely recognize MacArthur's declaration of an Open City and continued bombing military objectives. Many churches and schools, needless to say, were destroyed in the process

On Friday, January 2nd, 1942, late in the day around 6:00 P.M., the Japanese troops entered Manila, hesitating to do so earlier because of differing objectives from the Imperial Army. Should they first take Manila or push on to Bataan? Manilans able to sleep that night awoke January 3rd to see the Japanese flag flying over every building that had previously flown the Philippine banner. Japanese sentries were posted two by two at every main street intersection and in front of clubs, hotels and apartment houses. On January 4th, the Manila *Tribune* carried an announcement from the Japanese Imperial Command that the sovereignty of the United States "had completely disappeared." Martial law was now established. And the announcement further exclaimed that the Philippines was emancipated from the "oppressive domination" and would now be established as a part of the "Co-Prosperity Sphere in Greater East Asia." The declaration went on to warn the populace, "Anyone who inflicts, or attempts to inflict, an injury upon Japanese soldiers or individuals shall be shot to death." And if the assailant could not be found the Japanese "would hold ten influential persons as hostages".

On the same day as that announcement, the Japanese officers, accompanied by civilian Japanese interpreters, conducted wholesale door-to-door searches and rounded up all enemy aliens—mostly Americans—breaking up families with Filipino mothers or fathers and told them to pack blankets and enough food for three days. Little did these people know they would be incarcerated for three years. They were thrown into the camp without the most basic necessities—without clothing other than what they had on, without bedding, without food and without money. Their homes had been looted and their businesses destroyed. Many were ill, and all were worried. They were thankful to still be alive, but even that seemed uncertain, and although some had their families together, others did not.

For each and every one of these people, the world had turned upside down, and their protection by the nation they believed to be the most powerful on earth had failed them. The Americans in STIC were the first in the proud history of their nation to be thrown *en masse* into an enemy concentration camp and denied the liberties they considered their birthright. They had witnessed their flag hauled down, and many, with dread, recalled the rape of Nanking where the Japanese butchered an estimated 150,000 male "war prisoners," massacred an additional 50,000 male civilians, and raped at least 20,000 women and girls of all ages, many of whom were mutilated or killed in the process. The internees were terrified and realized that they were at the mercy of an oppressive Oriental power. Presumably to quell their fears, the Japanese declared that the internees were being held in "protective custody" and that they were not prisoners of war. Laughably, the question was from what and from whom were they being protected? The same basic procedure may have occurred in Iloilo City, but the Carrolls, hiding in the jungle, missed that ignominy.

Three hundred men, women and children were the first internees to arrive at STIC on January 4th, and amidst much confusion were assigned to ten rooms on the second floor of the Main Building. Men and women were separated, and married couples were not allowed to stay together. It was utter chaos, which only got worse very quickly. Within *ten* days there were over 3,000 people in the camp, some 2,000 of whom were lodged in the Main Building, 700 in the gymnasium (all men) and 400 in the annex (women and children). Initial accounts depict people sitting around safeguarding suitcases if lucky enough to have been allowed to bring one, dazed and bewildered. Inside the building the hallways were overflowing with jumbled men and women and screaming children, all bumping into one another. People staked their "place" under tables, under stairways, on stairway landings, on laboratory benches, and on patches of plain concrete floors.

Thirty to fifty to sometimes eighty people were crammed into each room, with the average floor space per person a mere twenty-two square feet. In some rooms it was as low as sixteen square feet. In Hartendorp's book, one woman recalled that the Japanese soldiers put her and 70 others—51 women and 19 babies—into one room. "Incredibly there was no hysteria. One woman stood against a wall and sobbed, but later became the most helpful one in the room." Cots, in rooms that had them, were squeezed together four abreast with roughly a two-foot space between them for navigation. The general mix of this mass of humanity was 70% American, 25% British, and the remainder a mix of other nationalities—Danish, Polish,

Spanish, Mexican, Cuban, Russian, Welsh, Chinese, Swedish and Burmese.

With such a rapid influx of internees, pressing problems immediately arose. The Japanese realized the camp was in serious need of organization.

78

Chapter VII

Organization of STIC

Additional people were arriving daily at the internment camp, and the confusion and disorder were difficult to control. The Japanese Commandant, Lieutenant Hitoshi Tomayasu, asked the people if they had a leader, and it was decided that the role should fall to a business executive named Earl Carroll (of no relation to Norwood) who was the chairman of the South Malate District for the American Red Cross. Ernest Stanley, a British missionary who had lived several years in Japan, was then appointed as an interpreter. Interestingly, Stanley was regarded by many in the camp with suspicion and was generally disliked—they thought he was a British secret agent.

Earl Carroll had an enormous task before him. As general chairman, he appointed nine men he knew to form an Executive Committee. Their initial job was to create numerous sub-committees and appoint managers for every aspect of this new and complex organization. Like a city council, they had offices and kept minutes. The committees named were: Medical Service, Sanitation and Health, Work Assignment, Education, Recreating, Building and Construction, Release, Discipline, Religious Service,

Library, Fire Prevention, Vegetable Garden, Census, Lost and Found, Suggestions and Complaints, and Public Relations. Every base was covered! These committees took time to create and certainly not all were formed immediately. But in a sense, Carroll's job was comparable to creating the government of an international city, and the problems were colossally complex. People were hungry, and people were ill. Fortunately, the STIC populace had many of the most prominent people in the country—government officials, business executives, professional men, and experts in almost every field of activity. The general intelligence and level of ability was high, but harnessing that expertise was somewhat protracted. Pressing problems were many and deciding which were to be addressed first was thorny—exceedingly so.

Which nightmare was the most important—feeding the masses or housing them? Cramming 3,000 internees *(This number eventually grew to more than 4,000.)* into the university buildings was a horrific undertaking. One account by Tressa Cates in her memoir *Drainpipe Dairy* describes the confusion when everyone was jockeying for position.

I will long remember my first night at Santo Tomás. Throughout the night, Japanese soldiers flashed lights at us as they barked restrictions or orders through an interpreter to late arrivals. Although we were already crowded, more people continued to join us. Frightened children screamed and cried in their sleep, and the eleven-month old baby near my corner wailed most of the night. On top of the noise, confusion and glaring lights, we were chewed by bedbugs and mosquitoes.

Citizens of every stripe and social strata were all now squeezed together on equal footing. It had to be a veritable clinic for observing human nature and the social leveling that occurred. Earl Carroll's Executive Committee appointed monitors for each room. These "room leaders" supervised each living area, maintained discipline, organized people for roll-call *(The Japanese demanded such each morning and night and required everyone to bow low before the Commandant as his/her name was called.)*, and oversaw the recruitment of those needed for physical labor. All able-bodied persons were given a job. Former CEOs of industry held jobs on latrine detail, or as gardeners or carpenters. High society women dirtied their hands. From Frederic Stevens' *Santo Tomás Internment Camp* comes the following account:

So, it happened that the vice-president and general manager of a large electric supply house could be seen daily in one of the toilets, gravely handing out four sheets of toilet paper to which each internee was entitled. The president of the largest commercial firm in the Philippines became a guard and attendant in a toilet; the manager of an import and export concern of Manila sweated in digging drainage ditches; a bank manager volunteered to wash dirty, bedbug-infested mosquito nets, and did so for months; a well-known society lady of Manila took care of washing a certain sanitary necessity for women.

Bathrooms and showers were in ridiculously short supply. There were only four toilets and one basin for 400 women on one floor in the Main building, and no showers. Early on the stench of urine, feces, and also vomit had to be overwhelming. Earl Carroll, through his many Filipino connections outside the camp, procured necessary plumbing equipment for his sanitation committee to build additional facilities, and they also supplied tubs and taps outside for the women to wash their hair and clothing. This undertaking naturally took time, but no one had an inkling of how long they were going to be captive, so time was irrelevant.

Maintaining sufficient sanitation was a constant struggle, not only in providing additional showers, toilets, kitchen and dishwashing facilities, but also in the vigorous campaign against flies, mosquitos and rodents. Rats and snakes, including cobras, were trapped and killed. Open sewers were drained into the city's underground system. Trenches were dug at the rear of the grounds for trash. None of it could be hauled away because of Japanese refusal to let any trucks into the compound. Creative sorts 'manufactured' wire fly-traps that were hung on each garbage can, and awards were given to boys who killed the most flies each week. Mosquitos were somewhat controlled with spay guns in each room and the constant clearing of the drains and brush. Bed bugs were a terror and mattresses were dragged out on the lawn and constantly cleaned to little avail. Twice a day the rooms were swept; once a week they were emptied and the floors scrubbed clean with disinfectant. The university was undoubtedly cleaner than ever before.

Emergency water supply was maintained using the Main Building's 50,000-gallon capacity roof-tanks and the 500,000-gallon swimming pool. Everyone needed to work, not only for practical reasons—there was much to do—but also for morale. Stevens also remarked in his book referenced above:

Internment, when continued over a long period of time, has a sort of deadening effect on the mind; ability to concentrate diminishes, people become irritable, ready to squabble over trifles. But thanks to the varied nature of camp life, and above all, thanks to the ability to work, the morale of the Camp remained high throughout the duration of internment

A socialistic principle was first put into effect: "From every man according to his ability; to every man according to his need", but it could not support itself.

Feeding more than 3,000 people was difficult and *adequate* feeding was an impossibility. The Red Cross, which could have eased the overwrought conditions in the beginning, was severely handicapped because the managers and chairmen of the Philippine and American divisions were internees. Additionally, many Red Cross supplies were confiscated by the Japanese, and the fact that this was a heinous violation of international conventions was completely ignored. A crude sign posted in English read: "Internees in this camp shall be responsible for feeding themselves."

Consequently, the first effort at feeding the masses was through the operation of a small student canteen on the campus with food that was purchased on the open market by a committee of buyers escorted by Japanese soldiers. Service, of course, left much to be desired as one could easily stand in line for more than an hour before moving into the small dining area and then hurriedly devouring his food to make room for those waiting behind. Breakfast was a plate of cracked-wheat porridge, a roll and a cup of black coffee. Dinner was a small portion of stew or a sardine, a roll, a cup of tea and a banana for dessert. Occasionally there was macaroni and a rice pudding for dessert. It wasn't very much, and it wasn't very good, but there was, at least, a modicum of nutrition. Leading members of Manila's society stood in line with everyone else, week after week, month after month with their one tin plate in hand—social leveling in action.

As provisions for so many proved vexingly inadequate, the Japanese finally allowed the Red Cross to install a field kitchen in the Annex and another one at the "hospital." The hospital, which was crafted with tents that arrived from the outside, was an effort by the internees and the Red Cross to create a 100-bed facility—again pitifully inadequate.

Getting food to the camp had its own difficulties. As mentioned earlier, buyers were allowed to leave the camp on passes, wearing red arm bands to identify them as enemy aliens, and scour the markets every day to find enough food. But by March, imports from Allied countries were cut off, so no milk, butter, or flour were available at any price. Everything, then, was locally produced—vegetables, rice, fruit and carabao meat. Transporting it to the camp held its own perils as trucks and fuel had to be procured, and then predatory Japanese soldiers had to be dealt with. Many times, rice, milk and cracked wheat, which the internees liked the best, were commandeered, but such highway robbery was only a small part of Japanese pilfering of Manila after the occupation.

Because of the difficulties in supplying food, be it the Red Cross or the food committees allowed to scour the markets, the camp would have starved had it not been for "The Gate". This remarkable phenomenon, also known as "The Fence" and "The Package Line," started early on. Peddlers stood outside the iron gate selling food and all manner of necessary articles. Faithful Filipino servants, neighbors and friends came too, bringing food, bedding and clothing. They would shout the names of their friends or employers and push baskets of food, thermoses of hot coffee, milk, bananas, and bundles of clean laundry, through the gate, laughing and crying and making inquiries. Internees with such friends were lucky. It is anyone's guess if Norwood might still have had friends in Manila that helped him or even knew he was there.

The Japanese couldn't understand this show of loyalty and affection by the Filipinos for their "oppressors" and attempted to drive them away with sticks and batons. But those faithful friends kept coming back. After about the third week, the Commandant issued an order forbidding such deliveries.   When Earl Carroll came to ask why, the Commandant explained that he couldn't stand to see the internees fed through the bars of the fence "as if they were animals". Also, he had complaints from Japanese, Germans and Italians who passed by the fence saying such freedom of the internees made the place look like a "picnic ground".

Carroll and his committee had a ready proposal. They suggested that the fence be screened with sawali (*woven split bamboo*) matting to prevent outside observation and that those bringing packages be allowed to come through the gate at certain hours of the day in an orderly fashion. After deliberation, the order was rescinded and the faithful continued to come every day, month after month—about *900 of them* a day.

Friends, family and servants came through the gate and deposited the packages at four long tables. Sabered Japanese officers inspected the packages for "contraband" such as weapons, flashlights (possible signaling devices), liquor and notes. The internees selected to work the detail took the packages further back on the lawn and arranged them in alphabetical order.   Shouting or waving was prohibited, but the people learned to signal each other in creative other ways—bobbing up and down on their toes, scratching their heads or waving their elbows. After the

Filipinos left, the internees were allowed to approach in a line and receive their package as their name was called. The Package Line hours became the principal social time for the internees, not only to see someone from outside the camp, but also to talk amongst themselves. There was not a soul in camp that was not deeply touched by the amazing generosity, loyalty and affection shown by the Filipino friends and servants.

Further ideas for feeding the camp came in the establishment of a food-exchange and camp store. Earl Carroll's Central Committee got approval from the Commandant to allow the Army and Navy Y.M.C.A. to bring in canteen supplies, and a drug company and milk plant to bring in toilet articles, notions, tobacco and milk. The plan was to also give internees a way to exchange food items they may have too much of for something they needed. A 10% commission was levied to form a relief fund for indigent internees who had no friends or contacts. All of these ideas were going quite well until a Japanese interpreter, who could see an opportunity for personal gain, obtained permission to establish a sandwich, coffee and ice-cream stand. Another Japanese civilian opened a cigar, cigarette and candy stall. The Commandant, with relish, then informed the Executive Committee that *their* camp store must close. Truly, the frustration had to be overwhelming for the committee members who worked nonstop to organize the feeding programs, but at least the food-exchange was, in part, still carried out at the rear of the main building.

A shrewd Filipino businessman was granted a concession for an order-branch in the lobby of the main building whereby orders for department-store articles were taken and deliveries made the following day. What an amazingly convenient source for providing necessities and occasional pleasures for those who had money. That 10% relief fund levy was always added to all the orders.

The early difficulties of accessing services of the Red Cross slowly started to ease because of the constant posturing and bargaining of the Central and Executive Committees. Eventually the Red Cross not only paid for all the food consumed, but also all the equipment and supplies used for kitchen, hospital, toilet and bath installations, and medical supplies. More than 2,000 beds and cots plus clothing for needy internees were secured, over and above that provided by the Package Line. Even though accessing funds from the Red Cross deposits at the Philippine National Bank for such provisions was constantly a struggle (the Japanese, for the most part, closed down the banks), a loan from a wealthy internee would often suffice. *Slowly* the bare necessities for making internment bearable began to materialize. "City government" was taking hold.

Name	Sex	Nat.	Age	Location		
Brown, Eva F.	F	Am	40	KY	"	"
Brown, Frankworth	M	Am	33	Gym	"	"
Byrd, Henry Purret	M	Am			"	"
Carr, Henry	M	Am	39	Gym	"	"
Carroll, Norwood M.	M	Am	34	Annex	"	"
Carroll, Isabel	F	Am		Annex	"	"
Carroll, Norwood Lee	M	Am		Annex	"	"
Carroll, Mary Margaret	F	Am	3	Annex	"	"
Carroll, William Singleton	M	Am	1	Annex	8	"	"
Cassanave, Emilio	M	Am	36	Gym	"	"
Cassanave, Greta	F	Am		54	"	"
Cassanave, Pedro, Jr.	M	Am	32	Gym	"	"
Cassanave, Maria	F	Am	34	15	"	"
Cassanave, Theodore	M	Am	46	Gym	"	"
Cassanave, Peter	M	Am	8	Gym	"	"
Casay, John V.	M	Am	30	Gym	"	"
Cassanave, Olive	F	Am		54	"	"
Cassanave, Pedro	M	Am	76	Camp Hosp.	"	"
Chambers, R. Fred	M	Am	40	Gym	"	"
Chambers, Dorothy Joy	F	Am	40	Annex	"	"
Chambers, Carol Joy	F	Am	4	Annex	"	"
Churchill, George N. W.	M	Br	36	Gym	"	"
Churchill, Irene W.	F	Br	30	49A	"	"
Dekin, A. Charles	M	Am	81	Gym	"	"
Dekin, N. Ross	F	Am	41	49A	"	"
Deegan, Stephen	M	Br	26	Gym	"	"
Davies, Wallace	M	Br	45	Gym	"	"
Davies, Elizabeth Ann	F	Br	44	Camp Hosp.	"	"
Davies, Lawson Ingram	M	Br	9	Gym	"	"
Dewhurst, Maria D.	F	Br	35	Camp Hosp.	"	"
Emerson, Ause	M	Am	68	EB 108	"	"
Ernst, Flora O.	F	Am	48	58A	"	"
Fortune, Elijah	M	Am	64	EB lobby	"	"
Fleming, Jackson	M	Am	56	Gym	"	"
Friederichsen, Paul D.	M	Am	35	Gym	"	"
Friederichsen, Kathleen	F	Am	32	Dorm	"	"
Friederichsen, Douglas	M	Am	9	Gym	Iloilo City	
Friederichsen, Robert	M	Am	8	Dorm	"	"
Greenbaum, William E.	M	Am	45	Gym	"	"
Greenbaum, Mary Maynard	F	Am	42	54	"	"
Harris, Ruth L.	F	Am	44	52	"	"
Hinkley, Helen	F	Am	57	52A	"	"
Linden, Francisco Antonius Van der	Male	Dutch	31	Gym	"	"
Hodges, Linnie	F	Du	40	Gym	"	"
Hof, Adrianus Teunis van't	M	Swiss	24	Gym	"	"
Iller, Max	M	Du	33	Gym	"	"
Jacobs, Andreas Cornelius	M	Du	57	Camp Hosp.	"	"
Janssen, Wilhelmus Franciscus	M	Du	58	Gym	"	"
Kamp Van de Everherdus	M	Br	40	Gym	"	"
Kerr, Ivan Wallace	F	Br	31	Annex	"	"
Kerr, Dorothy Beatrice	F	Br	4	Annex	"	"
Kerr, Cynthia Margaret	M	Br	2	Annex	"	"
Kerr, John Wallace	M	Du	40	Gym	Iloilo City	
Kest, Cornelius	M	Du	30	Gym	"	"
Koelman, Cornelius J.	M	Am	29	Gym	"	"
Lee, James Milton	F	Am	50	Annex	"	"
Lee, Marguerite	M	Am	2-1/3	Annex	"	"
Lee, Elfred Milton	M	Am	1-1/8	Annex	"	"
Lee, David James	M	Am		Camp Hosp.	"	"
Loring, Gregorio M.	F	Am	19	46	"	"
Loring, Lourdes	F	Am				
Loring, Concepcion			(conti...)			

Internee list at Santo Tomás with two other families
from the jungle

91

Aerial view of Santo Tomás

92

The Main Building and the Education Building

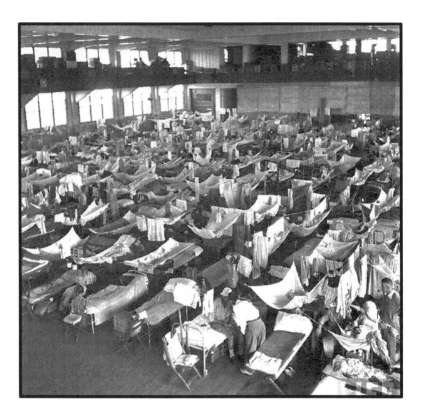

Crowded gym conditions. Norwood was here.

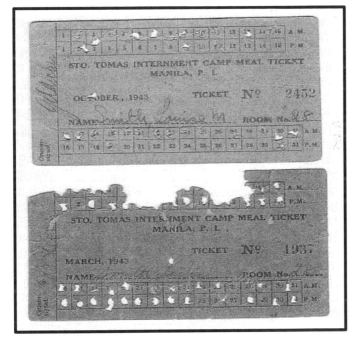

Meal tickets

The Package Line

The Front Gate area

Washing Clothes

Internees greeting outsider

Chapter VIII

Life in General

As the early chaos began to settle, the internees had to find ways to battle the boredom and monotony of being imprisoned. As mentioned earlier, chores were taken up. People were not only mopping floors and scrubbing toilets but also mowing lawns, cleaning drainage gutters and generally keeping busy. Creative types rose to the top with ideas that developed camaraderie and wide-ranging goodwill. Peter Wygle, in his book *Surviving a Japanese P.O.W. Camp,* relates how is father Robert became quite the camp handyman. It was by kindly relieving an older man who was trying to burn a pile of trash that Robert unwittingly took over the camp "garbage duty" job. He recalled how amazed he was by the stuff that people threw away, intentionally or otherwise. Being a bit of a pack rat, Robert sorted through the piles and set up a table with things that people might be able to use. In his words:

I buried all the camp garbage, for 4,000 people, alone. After a day or two, I began to be struck by people's wastefulness and foolishness. I was also amazed at the ignorance of my own people. I had always thought that

Americans were clever and resourceful, but the garbage job convinced me that Americans were dumb—and the Englishmen were dumber. Soon I combined the garbage job with a salvage operation and supplied many people with things that others threw away. Silverware, jars, tableware, kindling, wire, nails, bottles, jugs, cartons, shoes, tin containers, wrapping paper, thermos bottles, spare parts, rags, clothes—all of this came my way, and I kept a "help yourself" pile in the shade of a tree.

It *is* curious that so much was discarded, but space, undeniably, was at a premium, and the wealthier internees were getting a lot of things through the Package Line. Robert became the busiest man in STIC with his repairs and creations—all to the internees' benefit (*Robert was the mastermind behind the garbage fly traps.*). One thing he masterfully created were knitting needles. When he grudgingly made a set for one internee, a rush of women descended upon and begged him to make more. Knitting was a blessed pastime for many, and Robert's wife knitted constantly. When yarn ran out, she would knit with white and colored grocery twine. "You haven't lived until you've sat on a wooden bench for several hours with your bony bottom encased in skivvies knitted out of twine," Peter Wygle said in his book. "I probably have a knit-two, purl-two pattern etched on my fanny to this day."

By the third week of internment, social functions began to materialize. One internee, Dave Harvey, arose quickly as a gifted emcee—putting on stage and radio shows, skits and plays—almost from the very beginning of internment. Tressa Cates in *Drainpipe Diary* described the first gathering held on January 19th:

Almost 500 of the internees spread grass mats on the west patio of the Main Building for a community sing-along. The walls of this old Spanish university resounded to the lovely strains of "Old Kentucky Home," "Sewanee River,' "When Irish Eyes are Smiling," and other favorites. Songs of a patriotic nature were not permitted by order of the Commandant.

Professional entertainers saw no reason to let internment stifle their creativity. Costumes, a stage, and stage scenery were crafted. Variety shows with instrumental and vocal performers, magicians, quiz shows, sword swallowers, you name it, were presented every Saturday and drew large crowds. And when one was in progress, the area was called "The Little Theater Under the Stars." Spectators either sat on the ground or enjoyed "loge-styled" seats in the second and third story windows. Harvey's team used a broadcast system built by one of Manila's best-known radio technicians to broadcast plays comparable to the ones

101

enjoyed before the war. The Music Committee picked selections from a library of 3,000 records, including country and western, big-band dance tunes, and arias from famous operas for internee enjoyment. The camp knew when the Japanese were angry with them: the music stopped. A nurse in STIC recounts in the Hampton Union news, a Portsmouth, New Hampshire rag:

On Christmas 1943, the "Messiah" was presented by a group of internees with a 100-voice chorus and a large orchestra. The instruments for the orchestra came from the junior symphony orchestra of the high school in Manila and from the Manila symphony orchestra. Since there was little or no privacy for anyone anywhere in camp, the rehearsals were held on the roof of the camp in a futile attempt to make the presentation a surprise. The members of this company particularly enjoyed the "Hallelujah Chorus." Soon fellow internees began to look forward to the Christmas season passing for they said one more Hallelujah would have been too much. (*Does this sound familiar? This version of the Hallelujah chorus was probably a bit better than the version the Carrolls heard at the Iloilo camp with a single reed organ and accordion the year before*)

A garden was established. The crew assigned to that job—priests, bankers, and engineers among them—turned a junkyard swamp of cogon grass in the rear of the campus into a five-acre vegetable plot that helped feed the internees for most of the internment. The garden was tilled and tended until the last days of camp with approval, of course, from the Japanese who did little to feed anyone.

Sports were quickly established for all who wished to participate including soccer, baseball, field hockey, croquet, football and basketball. Leagues were formed and given names matching the pro teams at home in the U.S. Peter Wygle, who was eleven years old when interned, tells the story of a hilarious baseball game with the Japanese soldiers (*Baseball wasn't actually played—softball was the game*):

Probably the classic sports story to come out of the camp is the one where the Japanese commandant wanted to pit his guards against one of our better teams. I think they came out in uniforms and full gear. They looked great, but MAN did they stink as baseball players. The third baseman would boot a dribbling ground ball, then pick it up and throw it all the way over the spectators behind first base. The Commandant (pitching, naturally) would go storming over all bluish yellow in the face, throw his glove at the poor guy, stick his face up against his and yell at him at the top of his voice for five minutes. Then he'd storm back to the pitcher's mound and start pitching overhand again. He wouldn't pitch softball-style (underhand), so the camp wags started the story around that the Commandant had been told, "play ball with the prisoners and don't try anything underhanded."

Our people were playing like a bunch of jelly-boned goons, trying not to beat the guards by more than about 450 to nothing, because they figured that would be akin to beating the boss at golf.

And speaking of golf, a three-hole golf course was maintained for a while, and one of the camp nurses recalled having learned the game while at STIC. An intramural tournament was even held, and golf clubs were handed over the fence by servants of those who had them at home. A veteran boxer was discovered in the camp and soon that sport flourished. Purposefully avoided by *all* internees were calisthenics, not surprising since the Japanese avidly recommended them.

Bridge, chess, cribbage, pinochle: these were the games offered to those averse to sports. Poker was played nearly every night in the Gymnasium, but the games never became raucous because there was little money to bet and no booze to drink.

"Barn dances" were organized for teenagers for a time, but the Japanese disallowed ballroom dancing as too sexually explicit. Square dancing was okay. Socialization for the teens was difficult because any show of affection— holding hands or kissing and embracing—was strictly forbidden. Rules for teens were a slippery slope—most of the them were systematically and creatively broken—but then such is the normal behavior of teens everywhere. School was more than likely the main place to gather and communicate, and through assiduous efforts of the Education Committee, classes were established with internee teachers and professors holding courses in any building with available space.

From Frederic Stevens' book, *Santo Tomás Internment Camp,* comes the following:

O July 7, the Education Department announced that its curricula now included 46 college-level classes, including Japanese, Tagalog, French, etymology, calculus, philosophy, history, and several business-education courses. The camp high school enrolled 130 students, and the elementary and middle school (first through eighth grades)198. Business and college classes enrolled almost 600 adults in 1942. The high school curriculum included English, Algebra, General Sciences, Latin, French, Spanish, Biology, Plane Geometry, World History, Chemistry, Trigonometry, Solid Geometry, American History 1500-1900 A.D., Physics, and Economics.

Diplomas were created that the students could use to vouch for their education when they returned to the U.S. and other countries. Two libraries were assembled from donations, one for elementary and middle-school students and the other for high-school students and adults. STIC internees also had access to two other large libraries, making them possibly the most book-flush prisoners of WW II. However, maps were not allowed to be used, and as the war wore on, a shortage of paper made it extremely difficult to conduct classes and assignments.

Bobbie Olson, a friend of the Carrolls, who was thirteen when interned, remembers saving the report cards from her time in school. When asked years later at a STIC reunion in Las Vegas if she had a romance while interned, she said no. As a beautiful young teenage girl, did she ever remember feeling afraid of being harassed by a Japanese guard? Again, she said, "No, never. The Japanese apparently didn't like the scent of American women." That is not to say that there was no flirting among the girls and the soldiers, because there was *(and the offenders were categorically rebuked by the Executive Committee)*. But it was fortunate that the atmosphere of the camp was not predatory, at least for American women.

Unlike other prison camps with only men, the presence of women and children at STIC did much to brighten the living conditions. Although they added to the responsibilities of camp management and surely to every man, the life of the men was certainly nearer to normal than it would have been without them. The Japanese are characteristically fond of children and the guards did their best to make friends with them. Although the parents did not look upon this with favor, it promoted better relations, unquestionably, between the internees and the Japanese authorities.

The children lost their fear of the soldiers. From Hartendorp's account:

One day, a new group started a machine-gun drill on the campus, rushing forward, dropping to the ground, setting up their gun, then jumping up and running forward again— perhaps to impress the internees with the "reality of their situation." But this grim effect was entirely spoiled by a large group of children who rushed across the campus behind the soldiers, shouting and laughing and imitating them. The soldiers soon stopped these exercises.

How in the world did 4,000 people from every conceivable walk of life and differing cultures manage to co-exist at STIC? There were great contradictions in human nature. The rich "big shots" were often weak and scared while the lower-class population, used to hard work and privation, took the difficulties in stride. There were crooks and thieves and those who kowtowed to the Japanese. There were those who got rich off profiteering and those who grew poor giving to those in need. But all in all, life at STIC was an amazing testimony to the human condition and how man adapts to his circumstances. Attitude was everything. Those accustomed to freedom and autonomy had difficulty with imprisonment and complained daily while others knuckled down and realized they had to make the best with what they had. No less important, unquestionably, were the organizational efforts of the Executive Committee to make an untenable situation more tolerable. For a period, at least at the beginning, there was a measure of stability.

Children enjoyed mimicking the soldiers drills

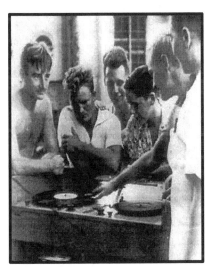 

Scenes in the camp

More camp scenes

Chapter IX

The First Executions

STIC had been up and running for two months, struggling to find a rhythm and sense of order, when three men did a desperate and reckless thing. On February 12th, two Englishmen and an Australian, at eight o'clock in the evening, climbed over the fence and escaped. By two o'clock the next day, they were captured, brought back to camp and severely beaten by a squad of Japanese soldiers. Witnesses said the men were hardly able to walk. A notice, by order of Commandant Tomayasu, was sent out by the Executive Committee to the room monitors, to be read aloud to the internees. It read as follows:

We regret very much to report that three men escaped from Santo Tomás last night at 8 o'clock. They were apprehended today by Japanese soldiers and returned to camp where they were severely punished. Fortunately for them, they were brought back to the camp instead of being given the supreme penalty of death, the usual punishment for escapes. (*This was a lie, but the internees did not know it at the time.*)

They will be transferred to some other place. Representatives of the Executive Committee upon request of the Japanese authorities, visited them before their departure, at which time they asked that this message be sent to the internees: 'We deeply regret our actions. We know that we made a big mistake and we urge that no one ever attempt it again.'

The Commandant is very angry that his cooperation should have been requited in such a manner and has stated that any recurrence will result in death for the escapees and very stringent restrictions for the internees. It is therefore very important that each person interned here take every possible precaution to prevent another escape.

The Executive Committee,

EARLCARROLL, General chairman

The men were transferred to a jail, and ultimately were court martialed and sentenced to death by the High Command. Tomayasu had asked that the beating be punishment enough but was overruled. The following account was extracted from a series of articles by Earl Carroll that appeared in the Chicago Herald-American in August 1945.

"Every detail of the murder of three young Britishers of Santo Tomás by our Jap captors is as vivid in my mind this minute as if it had happened only an hour ago. You don't forget things like that—not when you see brave men buried alive and feel the breath of death as it whistles past your own head.

B.B. Laycock, Thomas Henry Fletcher, and H.E. Weeks were good men. They were young. They had the courage to dare. And they could not stand the thought of sitting out the war in a Jap internment camp.

We knew nothing of the escape until the middle of the next afternoon, when a squad of Jap MPs roared into the camp triumphantly returning the men.

The three were dumped into a room on the first floor of the main building and questioned. Tomoyasu, the commandant, was there. He wasn't as bad as he was weak. I suspect that Takahashi, the second in command, did most of the persuasive questioning. Afterwards, Tomoyasu sent for me and the two monitors of the rooms from which the men escaped. Tomoyasu remined me that he had warned the penalty for escape was death—and implied that I and the room monitors would suffer the same penalty as the escapees.

I then was ordered to see the three men. Takahashi had enjoyed himself. Laycock's face looked like raw hamburger. He tried to speak to me, but only a moan and a mumble came out. They were taken away and Takahashi assured us that the men were only being taken to another internment camp.

The next morning, I was informed a court martial had sentence the three to die. We decided to draft a petition to the commandant, and while working on it, a civilian interpreter broke into the meeting and declared that Tomayasu had tried to win leniency for the doomed men and had failed. We demanded a meeting with the commandant and the interpreter came back saying he was too broken up to talk about it.

Carroll went on in his article to explain how Tomayasu had sent word that he had done all he could, as an officer, to stop the execution. He would now humble himself and dress as an ordinary Japanese citizen to plead his case before the High Command. He did, indeed, emerge from his office in a kimono and wooden sandals, and drive off in his car, but he was returned unsuccessful. The harsh realities of internment came crashing down. Everyone in camp was stunned that these men were truly going to be shot. After all, the Japanese, themselves, had formally described the internees as 'civilians in protective custody.' To continue Earl Carroll's account:

Rumors flew everywhere...*they had already been executed, they had got a reprieve, the monitors were going to be shot, Carroll was going to be shot.* The last rumors were given real credence when Tomoyasu sent for Stanley (the interpreter), the room monitors and me. They piled us into cars and put a squad of soldiers into a bus.

We went to San Marcelino jail and the three prisoners were brought out. When they saw us, they began smiling. They thought they were going to go free. When we drove to the Chinese cemetery north of Manila and stopped near a large, freshly dug grave, they knew.

"Why, we haven't been tried!" exclaimed Laycock. The stuff we had been given about a court-martial was a Jap lie. Tomayasu asked me if I had anything to say to the men. I do not recall all that I told them, but I remember saying this: "Your names will not be forgotten at Santo Tomás. You are dying as martyrs to freedom." I gave each man a cigarette and started to light them. One of the Jap guards pushed me aside and lighted them himself.

Takahashi seated the three on the mound of earth beside the grave with their feet dangling in. Laycock, an Australian, refused to be blindfolded. "I'll die like a man, not a rat," he said. But Takahashi ordered him blindfolded anyway.

Then the Jap detail took up positions 15 feet in front of the men and took out their sidearms. Takahashi was grinning when he gave the order to fire.

Those pistols were small bore, and would kill a man only if the bullet struck a vital spot. The Japs could not aim that well. They fired and fired. I counted 13 shots. Weeks' body fell in last. Then the Japs stood over them, firing down into the grave. Groans were still coming from the grave when the Japs began to shovel dirt into it.

The Japs were still shooting when Tomoyasu turned away, mumbling to himself. He went behind a clump of bushes and looked the other way. Stanley told me Tomayasu was saying "It's butchery. They should have the proper instruments." Maybe he meant swords. Before the Japs were driven from Manila, they killed nearly 4,000 people at that cemetery. And most of the dead were beheaded.

As we left the scene, one of the Jap guards who had just been pumping bullets down into the grave was decorating it with bougainvillea. The next day, the executive committee read this into the minutes: "All three men faced their end bravely and heroically without faltering, and the committee wishes to record its admiration for their superb courage."

What more could we say?

It wasn't long after the executions that Lieutenant Hitoshi Tomayasu was promoted to the command of the gendarmerie of Greater Manila and was relieved by R. Tsurumi as Commandant of the camp. Tomayasu, 55 years old, spoke no English, and had initially taken a stern attitude in his leadership, but as time passed became somewhat more relaxed. Tsurumi was a civilian official who had completed consular and diplomatic service abroad, so he spoke English well and was more flexible, better able to understand the internee point of view, and more apt to take it into consideration. According to Hartendorp, when Tomayasu left camp, he was quoted in the *Internews* (the camp rag) as saying:

"When I first came to this camp I did not know what my feelings were toward the internees. I knew only that they were enemy nationals. My previous contact with foreigners was in Kobe and Shanghai, and I thought them proud and lacking in understanding of the Japanese. But since I have been here your cooperation and understanding have brought me a feeling of friendship which I had not thought possible under the circumstances. In the discharge of my duties here I have always had to work under orders from above. I appreciate your understanding of that situation. If the cooperation which has existed in this camp were possible on an international scale there would be no cause for international disputes. In past months other nations have misunderstood us and we have misunderstood them. I never expected that the affairs of this camp would go as smoothly as they have."

Though all the facts concerning the executions were not generally made known to the camp, the event brought crashing down the reality that no matter what their alleged status was as "internees under Japanese protection," they were *prisoners* and they were at Japanese mercy.

A Protestant memorial service for the men was held the following afternoon on campus, and the next morning a requiem mass was given in the Seminary chapel. Almost the entire camp attended despite or perhaps because the Commandant did not favor the conducting of the service.

According to Hartendorp's chronicle, the *Tribune* on February 16th carried the following announcement:

NOTICE
Thomas Henry Fletcher, English
Henry Edward Wynox, English
Brecky Brushwick Seacock, English

These three Britishers, together with other enemy nationals, have been interned on January 3rd, 1942. But of late, taking advantage of the generosity and good treatment which they were accorded by the Japanese Army, they have not only disobeyed orders and disrupted the peace of the camp, but they have also tried to communicate with the outside world for the purpose of giving information to the enemy. Lastly, they have tried to escape from the camp on the evening of February 11th, 1942. Therefore, they were court-martialed and shot to death in accordance with military laws.

The Command-in-chief
For the Defense of the
City Of Greater Manila

Chapter X

News Within the Camp

The second year of captivity, 1943, began with a sour but determined mood. The *STIC Gazette*, an internal newspaper of usually two mimeographed sheets of paper, decreed: "We don't need New Year's resolutions to help us carry on. We simply *will* carry on—steadily, bravely, a bit complainingly, perhaps, but proudly and honorably." How long was the war going to last? How *long* was this hideous internment to be endured? Boredom and impatient longing for release and freedom were the principal maladies of STIC, and the desire was fierce to see American planes overhead instead of the ones with red spots on the ends of the wings. But there was one conviction that did much to bolster the moral. Japan *would* be defeated in the end. When was anyone's guess, and estimates varied from a few months to a year or two, all depending on the information gleaned or rumors of the day.

Those accustomed to free press were vexed by the lack of dependable news. Copies of the *Manila Tribune,* which were naturally edited by the Japanese, were circulated in a limited number. And while the contents were known to be pure unadulterated propaganda, the ability to read between the lines grew strong. The claims of Japanese victories were depressing, but news of American successes cheered everyone. Some were true, and some were false, so as time passed people became critical and accepted the seemingly best authenticated reports cautiously. Some refused to listen or read anything, vowing to only believe American victory when they saw the planes with their own eyes.

At the core of human survival, there is often a measure of humor that serves as a coping mechanism. A few camp wits devised amusing reports for just that purpose such as: "Hundreds of American planes, launched from a submarine, landed at Mariveles," or "the Japanese told MacArthur: 'Surrender in 24 hours, or else we will!'" A few items were introduced as coming from "a fairly unreliable source."

Summaries of radio broadcasts were smuggled into camp by visitors or those out on temporary pass. The reports were claimed to have come from the "Voice of Freedom" or San Francisco or London. The Japanese did their best to interfere with broadcasts from abroad, and radio antennae were, of course, expressly prohibited in camp. If anyone was caught with even a scrap of electrical wire, it was a capital crime. But Yankee ingenuity was always at work.

Radio receivers and transmitters were constructed by a few internees, and one radio was brought into STIC in the camp electrician's luggage. He kept it bolted in a 5-gallon tin which he covered and sank in a well. He also kept a reserve radio in a pressure cooker.

A third radio was constructed from scratch. This account comes from Bruce Johansen's book *So Far from Home:*

Key to the radio's assembly was the knowledge and straight face of Luis de Alcuaz, a professor of sciences at Santo Tomás, and secretary to the rector at the University. Some of the materials came from the University physics laboratories; the rest were smuggled in by Alcuaz, in very small lots. Internee Delvin Axe (who had been a communications technician for Pan American Airways in Manila) constructed the radio, with help from another radio technician, Jerry Sams.

Construction of this radio set began about May 15, 1943, and continued several months, due to delays in acquisition of some materials, and the need to keep the work secret.

In a war memoir *Forbidden Family* by Margaret Sams, she wrote that her husband Jerry, mentioned above, was once asked by Filipino guerillas to help set up a radio station in the hills around Manila (*She doesn't say how that request was conferred.*).

121

With help from one of the camp doctors, Jerry faked an illness to get out of the camp and into Philippine General Hospital, from which he escaped for the hills. Jerry was out of camp for eight days, as several other internees covered for him. His absence was not detected by the Japanese.

When the radio was not being used, it was broken down into its component parts, split between three men and hidden securely. The Japanese suspected that there were secret radios in camp and searched diligently for them. Hiding places must have been very good because none were ever found, nor did the Japanese ever find a clandestine radio station that had begun broadcasting in or near Manila. "Radio Juan de la Cruz," the Filipino equivalent to John Doe, had shortwave links to the radio station KGEX in San Francisco, and internees in STIC could hear the broadcasts on their concealed long-wave sets. Radio Juan de la Cruz evaded Japanese detection for several months by frequently moving its transmission equipment around Manila.

Sketchy reports from outside the camp pointed to a possible rolling back of the Japanese tide of conquests. Yes, throughout 1942, the Americans *were* making successful inroads in the Pacific. The Battle of the Coral Sea took place in May; the Battle of Midway, the turning point of the Pacific Campaign, followed in June; Guadalcanal occurred in

August—all three conflicts bloody, grueling and hard-fought, but victorious nonetheless. Word leaked into the camp in August that President Roosevelt had made a speech declaring "The Philippines will be redeemed from the yoke of the Japanese." The *Manila Tribune*, an unlikely source, headlined: "Roosevelt Makes Another Promise."

The news that the camp radios were able to transmit gave hope and sometimes despair to the internees, but as with all things, knowledge is king, and even though the news was not always promising, it gave the internees a gauge for determining the extent of their imprisonment. And that was something they could maybe hang their hat on.

A note on the internal news rags: The STIC Gazette *and the* Internews *were newspapers written by internees and distributed free of charge. The* Internitis *was a private enterprise, averaging 20 pages per issue, that sold for fifteen cents. The Commandant suspended the* Internitis *on November 25, 1942 because of paper shortage and its frivolous use of the freedom of speech. The* STIC Gazette *ran out of paper in January 1943.*

Chapter XI

Shanty Town

Men and women were not allowed to stay together. This we know. As stated early on, the men were mostly housed in the gymnasium and the women, with children, in the Annex or dormitory rooms. But it wasn't long, early February 1942, before some of the men started to build little shanties on the university grounds. Scraps of lumber, pieces of tin, boxes, gunny sacks, matting and blankets—any material that could be found—became for all appearances the utmost in squalor, but for those crouching within it was a slice of home. The earliest structures were simply lean-tos, but as times passed they resembled traditional Filipino grass huts. Some of the more fortunate internees had pre-fabricated "knockdown" nipa huts with bamboo beams cut to specifications. Some were even completely assembled outside the camp and rolled through the main gate.

Naturally, the shanties provided a place to escape from the crowded living spaces and an opportunity for families to be together during the day. In short order these little "houses" mushroomed all over the campus and for a period were ignored by the Commandant and Executive

125

Committee. But late in February a unit of Japanese inspectors visited the camp and ordered all the shanties taken down. The reason given was that "immoral practices" had to be taking place in them.

The Executive Committee quickly pointed out that the shanties provided relief from the crowded spaces not only for those who had them, but also for those who remained in the buildings. Fortunately, a compromise was then reached in which no shanty could have sides—only roofs—so that surprise inspections could take place. The edict irked the internees especially since the structures became more "sophisticated" and more like home for those who lived there. Some structures were even raised on stilts for better air circulation and protection from monsoon-season floods. As with other STIC rules, the regulation was open to evasion and humorously called "No Sex in the Shanties" or "When in Shanties, Keep on Panties." During the rainy season, the Japanese did ultimately allow the shanty owners to close the vertical shutters to protect their belongings. One need only imagine the determined rush to those dwellings when the rains came.

Dirt paths between the shanties were given names. "Mayors," room monitors for the shanties, were elected in "districts." The names for the districts were marvelous:

Glamourville, Toonerville, Froggy Bottom, Jerkville, Over Yonder, Cottage Park, Jungletown, Shantytown, Palm Court. The district called Garden Court had the most pretentious homes. "Streets" had names closely related to their surroundings: Duck Egg Drive, Camote Ave, Tiki Tiki Road, Talinum Lane were a few near the camp kitchen (*Camote is a sweet potato, talinum a sort of green spinach-like vegetable that no one liked*). The streets in Glamourville were Tobacco Road, Broadway and 42nd Street, Montgomery, Market, MacArthur Drive and Hollywood Boulevard. During the rainy season they all became swampy mires, but no one seemed to care.

Shanty architects worked hard to embellish their basic structures. They made built-in cabinets, window seats, porches, ironing boards, beds and tables. According to Bruce Johansen in his book "*So Far from Home,*" one lady of distinction summoned her white-enameled garden table and chairs, complete with a large folding umbrella. On the table, she set china plates and cups in their proper places on a white tablecloth.

Curfew for vacating the shanties and returning to respective quarters was 7:30 p.m. until 6:30 a.m. the following morning. But because of the terrible crowding, the men were finally allowed to sleep alone in them.

Frederic Stevens, a definitive chronicler of camp life in *"Santo Tomás Internment Camp,"* remarked, "The first female that we know of to sleep in the shanty area was little Miss Joy Ann King, aged three, who, being red-headed and having a mind of her own, refused to leave her Daddy."

Soon after that, husbands and wives began to sneak into the shanties under the cover of darkness. By the end of 1942, the Commandant complained regularly that the internees were abusing the camp rules and warned them if they couldn't police themselves, the shanties would be destroyed. In January of 1943, four men were sentenced to thirty days in jail because their wives became pregnant. The Japanese made the internees build a jail for just that purpose. Some of the women argued they had become pregnant while out of the camp on pass, but the Commandant replied firmly that the law had earlier been laid down: "No make babies on pass."

Finally, after two years of prohibiting cohabitation without success the Japanese relented, and on February 1, 1944, allowed the husbands and wives to sleep together legally in the shanties. That order united 567 families. Norwood and Isabel, initially housed in the gymnasium and Annex upon arrival in 1943, were undoubtedly happy to be able to live together once again as a family in the shanty

Norwood built. For an article in the Durham Herald on May 26, 1945, Norwood described his shanty:

To escape the crowded "goldfish bowl" existence, Carroll joined the ranks of the more adventurous to build "our home" in what became the "Shanty Town" settlement. Cannily contrived of Nipa palm, bamboo, and salvaged lumber, the hut was tied together with vejuka (cord-like vine) and thatched over with grass. Native style, some 10 feet by 12 feet, its flooring hiked up on hutches, mats of sawali lined the walls and blinds protected the window spaces against tropical storms. Here for their prison duration, the Carrolls lived a "Crusoe" existence.

By September 1, 1944, 137 of approximately 1,300 women were pregnant. Seventy-five births were recorded at STIC from 1942-1945.

Shanties behind Education Building

Shanties inside the courtyards

Cooking at Shanties

A finer shanty—perhaps at Glamourville

Chapter XII

Things Start to Deteriorate

Little Billy and his family were "making do" at STIC. Upon their arrival in June of 1943, things were going fairly smoothly in the camp. The organization and general conditions were, for the most part, tolerable. There was moderately passable food, and the various activities, described earlier helped sustain the morale. Both Norwood and Isabel did their part to volunteer and keep a "stiff upper lip", but caring for Lee, Peggy and Billy, nutritionally and emotionally, was naturally their focus.

A vexing problem for Isabel, though, was the scarcity of soap. In the Raleigh, North Carolina News and Observer newspaper, June 17, 1945 is another snapshot of camp life:

A bar of soap coast $30! Thirty American dollars for one little cake of soap. But it was worth it to the Norwood Carrolls because that little bar of soap carried with it all the intangibles of the life from which they had been wrenched.

"I hadn't any idea that it was so hard to keep clean," Mrs. Carroll lamented. "In ordinary life you take soap and cleanliness for granted. But without soap, keeping clean is almost an impossible job. We spent what now seems an incredible amount of time trying to keep clean. It cost us a small fortune, too."

"Well, she would insist on putting a clean garment on the children every day," Carroll interposed with a grin.

"Somehow, I felt that I just had to," she said. "It was good for morale, and I felt that if we didn't try to keep up to the mark as much as we could, we'd all just be lost. Besides, crowded conditions in the camp gave rise to a lot of skin diseases and keeping clean was one way to avoid them."

Carroll said that once he managed to preserve a hotel-size of Life Buoy for 34 days. They even traded some of their limited supply of food from a Red Cross package for soap. "And oh, that was a hard thing to do," sighed Mrs. Carroll.

Isabel told a story of helping in the kitchen one day and having a feeling of intense disquiet. She could not quite describe what she was feeling to the other woman with her, but upon looking up, saw a large boa constrictor curled in the rafter above her. Not overly emotive in nature, Isabel's response in the telling of this tale of an utterly unnerving sight was a rather calm one. She claimed to have simply backed out of the kitchen. Ho hum, a dangerous snake in the kitchen. Carry on.

Stifling, tropical, summer months wore on and wore everyone down. Camp chores, gardening, cleaning and tidying, just *existing,* was beginning to get more difficult as food sources waned. By mid-July, to add even more to the incessant misery, rains that were unusually heavy flooded many people out of their shanties, especially those not built on lifters or platforms. The halls of the buildings were again crowded with too many people, screaming babies and sopping wet, steaming clothes. Repeatedly, these storms swamped the campus all summer long. But on November 14, 1943, a horrific typhoon, the worst ever recorded in the Philippine Islands, dumped 27 inches of rain on the compound, destroying the shanties, flooding the buildings and wiping away much-needed food supplies. Flood waters rose due to Manila's highest tides of the year, so deep in some areas it covered the makeshift bamboo floors with backed-up sewage four to six feet deep. Those marooned in their shanties were rescued by other internees who had turned their wrecked homes into bamboo rafts. Emily Van Sickle recalled in her book *Iron Gates of Santo Tomás*:

People rushed distractedly to their shanties, and many returned with piteous tales of roofs and sides torn away.... Food losses were appalling, especially of sugar, which had dissolved by the hundred kilos in flood waters. Substantial quantities of rice, cassava flour, and cornmeal were damaged beyond recovery, and many a can of kerosene, important both as fuel and light, had floated away during that horrible night.

Electricity failed during the storm, and sewage leaked into Manila's water supply. The windows in the crowded corridors and rooms of the campus buildings were tightly closed against the wind and driving rain. One can

135

only imagine the hot, sticky and stagnant air created by the smoke of the kerosene lamps, the candles and dank body heat. To add more misery to the beleaguered internees, the gas lines also failed, and the kitchen stoves were shut down.

Unbelievably, the Japanese had warned the Executive Committee to avoid panic in the camp by *not* revealing the coming storm's strength, and this failure deprived the enraged internees of the time to prepare. The food stores, alone, could have been saved.

Did Norwood lose his shanty? It is not known exactly when he built it. No family stories of the Carrolls' abode were ever shared, other than the article in the Durham newspaper. So, did they have a shanty during the massive typhoon, and if so how did it fare? If one existed, more than likely it was ruined. And because *no* shanty builder wanted to go back to the crowded conditions in the Gymnasium, it is a good bet that Norwood, along with the many other internees, did their level best to construct a new one. How utterly disheartened they all had to be.

The typhoon and its destruction of food supplies initiated a grave decline. Half of Manila's rice crop was destroyed, and the day after the storm passed, the camp ration was cut twenty percent. Only slowly did the ruined food stocks begin to reappear, but market supplies in town were ever dwindling. Sugar ration was reduced to one tablespoon per person per day when six months earlier, it had been four tablespoons per day. Coffee rations was also cut with a tea substitute being served on Tuesdays and Fridays. The daily diet "on the line" in the fall of 1943 *before* the typhoon was:

Breakfast: 1 cup tea substitute, 1 teaspoon of sugar, 1 large ladle of corn-meal mush
Lunch: 1 plate of mongo beans cooked with beef
Dinner: 1 plate of vegetable and beef stew, 1 cup banana, 1 cup unsweetened tea substitute

After the typhoon, by December 2nd, all sugar was gone, along with fats and oils. A few days later, meat, milk and bread vanished. Coffee, when available, continued to be rationed with the grounds being used and reused three and four times. Less and less food from friends and servants was coming through the Package Line, and meals from the food line were getting grim. The result of this grave lack of nutritional food was, of course, illness. Beriberi and dysentery were the most prevalent maladies. Beriberi, a deficiency of thiamine (vitamin B1), results in numbness of the hands and feet, increased heart rate, shortness of breath and swelling of the lower leg. As it progresses, the swelling moves upward to the torso and sometimes the face. Dysentery, a type of gastroenteritis, results in bloody diarrhea caused by several types of infections such as bacteria, viruses, parasitic worms, or protozoa. These illnesses had the perfect conditions in a perfect storm.

To supplement the meager food supply, Norwood and eleven other men, after seeking permission from the Executive committee and Commandant, formed a work detail to grow their own garden. Laboring in intense heat with extremely poor soil on a three-acre plot, the men did the best they could to supply a meager tablespoon of greens per person every other day (*this is unbelievable, was Norwood exaggerating?*). As Billy grew, due to the lack of milk and other key nutrients, he became very bow-legged. Norwood claimed that Billy was *so* bow-legged he couldn't stop a pig in a ditch! Finding humor in all things, good and bad, was Norwood Carroll's forte, and thank heaven for that. But the lack of solid, good nutrition was affecting not only the children—their need for critical vitamins and minerals being vital to the formation of their teeth, muscles and bones—but everyone in the camp as well.

Laboring in the camp garden

Scene in Manila after typhoon

Chapter XIII

Christmas of 1943

A month after the horrific typhoon, the Christmas season arrived. It was the first Christmas at STIC for the Carrolls and the second for those interned from the beginning. For morale, it was important, of course, for everyone in camp to make Christmas happen. As told in chapter seven, Dave Harvey organized a remarkable performance of the "Messiah" with a 100-voice chorus and full orchestra. But even such a remarkable feat did little to enliven the internees after losing so much in the typhoon. But calmly carrying on was a must.

Families, with help from friends outside the camp, made toys and gifts out of anything they could muster to give the children a small measure of joy. Stuffed animals and dolls, wooden blocks, and wooden cutout animals were created for infants and toddlers; pencils, crayons and notebooks were collected for older children. On Christmas Day, an internee got permission from the Commandant to go outside the gate to dress as Santa Claus. Later, when the gate opened, he arrived in full dress, but was disappointingly lacking a sled, reindeer, or toy sack. For some, there simply wasn't much to get excited about. Yes, there were toys—

lots of them, all laid out on long tables, but none of the "spirit" of the season was in evidence, according to Elizabeth Vaughn in her book *The Ordeal of Elizabeth Vaughn.* The following depicts her observation of the day:

Children followed curt directions of the Christmas Committee to line up according to ages and were ready to file by gift-laden tables silently and unemotionally at signal to march. Toys were handed to children by the committee members. Santa stood by a small table bearing a miniature two-foot-high Christmas tree and doggereled the internees as follows before the distribution of gifts began:

Next year I hope to see you
In your home or residence
And may we not meet again
Behind a sawali fence.

I had not heard a "Merry Christmas" all day, nor a word of the Christmas carols we associate with the day.

Not giving a whit about the children in camp, the Japanese thought, however, it would be kind and generous to bring the Christmas spirit to the lucky civilians of Manila who were now ending their second year under Nipponese occupation. A festive party that was to take place on Thursday afternoon, December 23rd, was advertised all over the islands, promising free food and toys for those who might not otherwise enjoy the season. Excited children gathered early at Malacañang Palace, Quezon's former

Presidential residence, but were made to wait in the blazing sun until 3:30 when the gates finally opened. To continue Vaughn's reflection:

A voice over a loudspeaker called for order and announced that the President of the Islands would give a speech of welcome. The last thing the tired children wanted was a speech, but two years of military regime have taught them something of the necessity of patience and obedience. Speeches, patriotic war speeches, and at last the prizes for which they had come, free toys and food. They came away from this affair with the cheapest of Japanese celluloid toys— small animals and dolls so poorly constructed that many were mashed in or dismembered before the children left the grounds. And the food for which they waited so patiently— candies or fruit? No, each child was handed a small bag of raw camotes (sweet potatoes). They went home angry, feeling they had been betrayed and deceived.

Even though Vaughn's outlook of the camp's valiant attempts to embrace the holiday spirit of Peace on Earth was depressing, especially coming at the end of a year that was beginning to break down on many levels, there *was* a bright spot: the arrival of Red Cross food parcels! Each internee, children included, received a package weighing 48 pounds of heaven-sent relief. Spam, corned beef, bouillon cubes, canned salmon, a full fat powered milk known as KLIM (*milk spelled backwards*), tinned butter, a few packets of sugar, chocolate, tooth powder, cigarettes, and small bars of soap were some of the luxuries within. The soap wrappers were printed with the acronym GAYLA, which some internees thought meant "Greetings All You Loyal Americans!" Vital medicines, vitamins, a small towel, wash cloth, and surgical instruments were also included. The Japanese apparently allowed these parcels into camp—*this time.*

The Red Cross, throughout the war, sent these relief packages to POWs in Europe and the Pacific. The prisoners in German concentration camps regularly received the packages, but those in the Pacific did not. The Japanese refused to cooperate with the Red Cross because they linked U.S. military prisoners of war and internee exchanges with the package aid to the captives. Because J. Edgar Hoover and General MacArthur objected furiously to the proposed prisoner exchanges, the Nipponese refused to allow the life-saving relief parcels into the camps. In fact, they simply confiscated them for themselves.

On December 16th, however, excitement erupted in the camp when a Japanese truck dumped the Red Cross packages inside the gate. In their current state of hunger, the thought of getting new and different foods and supplies was overwhelming. But then rage and indignation took over when the soldiers began breaking into the kits. The guards kicked and smashed the packages open, spilling canned goods, bayonetting packs of cheese and scattering supplies. Teresa Cates in her *Drainpipe Diary* recalls:

> A speechless and hate-filled audience looked on, helpless and powerless to stop them. An emaciated and anguished-looking mother with two skinny kids at her side burst into tears.

The soldiers then removed forty packs of cigarettes that were enclosed in each box. Chesterfields (*made by Liggett & Myers*), Camels, and Old Golds were confiscated because the labels on the Old Gold cigarettes were offensive to them. The labels read:

> FREEDOM
> Our heritage has always been freedom.
> We cannot afford to relinquish it.
> Our armed forces will safeguard that heritage
> If we, too, do our share to preserve it.

All the cigarettes, therefore, were removed as a penalty. A protest erupted immediately. Tobacco had been absent in the camp for quite some time, and Robert Wygle in his son Peter's book *Surviving a Japanese P.O.W. Camp* described it best.

> Tobacco and rumors were two things the Japs couldn't stop, although those sentries cut the tobacco down to almost

nil. People smoked leaves from bushes and garden plants, rolled in any old newspaper that could be found. Bibles went up in smoke in great quantities, since bible paper is good stuff for rolling cigarettes. I read more bible on my cigarettes than I'd ever read before in my life. I think I got through all of Matthew, Luke, John, and half of the next one.

When the Executive Committee delivered to the Commandant a formal written complaint addressed to the International Red Cross, he begrudgingly returned a portion of the cigarettes—forty-two packages to each adult and none to children. There were more than 1200 children in camp, so the forty packs that had been included in their relief packs were enjoyed not by the men and women, but by the soldiers. The comfort that those cigarettes provided was terribly important for so many of the men and women who had an aching addiction. It also tempered the pain of hunger. And for those who didn't smoke, the cigarettes were a useful bartering tool.

So thrilling was the spectacle of fare not seen in over a year that many people dove into those boxes, ravenously gorging on the foods and sugar they sorely missed, while others stored the greater part under their cots—guarding it like treasure—not knowing when or if another relief package would come.

And naturally, a market for each commodity quickly arose. Corned beef sold for $11, a chocolate bar for $10, and an entire kit $750. Emily Van Sickle wrote in *Iron Gates of Santo Tomás:*

One internee, Hank Parfit, reaped profits that were staggering. He had become such a usurious merchant that his name had become a noun in the STIC vocabulary. If an internee took unfair advantage in trading because of scarcity, he was said to be "Parfiteering.

The celebration of Christmas was unquestionably different for everyone in the camp. Elizabeth Vaughn's was gloomy, but Emily Van Sickle's was anything but. From her aforementioned book she writes of a private feast that had been ordered at great expense from the outside:

Our plates were piled high with turkey, dressing, gravy, baked ham, potatoes, several vegetables, cranberry sauce, pickles...rice bread and butter...ice cream and cake. I had some guilt for the people without money to whom a taste of meat in the food line was an infrequent treat.

Infrequent treat? How about *no* treat? Granted, camp life was not entirely a socialistic endeavor. It basically was each man for himself, with the help of camp organization, but there is no doubt that many people sacrificed from time to time for his fellow internee. What a sorrowful example of how wealth that is not shared can be so cruel. One can hardly imagine how anyone within sight of this indulgence must have felt. But such is the reality of any society. Billy Carroll and his family surely had no such elaborate meal. Once, Norwood stated that a can of Spam, for five people, lasted three meals. It was a blessing the relief packages came when they did.

A disheartening edict from the Commandant further dampened spirits of everyone on Christmas Day. He refused to allow visits from friends and relatives outside the camp, his rational being that such visits, which had been allowed the year before, were "impractical." Many people who were turned away left weeping, taking with them thousands of packages of gifts and food for their loved ones. "Merciless and mean" only barely describes the actions taken that day by the camp director. It is not known if Norwood had any friends left in Manila that were turned away.

Yet, an entry in the camp log by Frederic Stevens in *Santo Tomas Internment Camp* said:

"The year 1943 ended in much better condition than might be expected under the circumstances. Most of the internees were losing weight, but otherwise relatively healthy. Food was very plain, but adequate."

As it happened the delivery of the Red Cross relief packages predated little Billy's second birthday by two

148

weeks. Maybe he got a little surprise, perhaps a small piece of chocolate to celebrate his big day.

Red Cross Relief Package

PRISONERS OF WAR BULLETIN

Published by the American National Red Cross for the Relatives of American Prisoners of War and Civilian Internees

VOL. 2, NO. 12   WASHINGTON, D. C.   DECEMBER 1944

The 1944 Christmas Package

Christmas Package No. 2, packed by women volunteers in the Philadelphia Center during the hottest days of the summer, reached Germany via Sweden in time for distribution to American prisoners of war and civilian internees held by Germany.

The first thousand Christmas packages sent in 1943 for American prisoners of war and civilian internees in Europe were hardly sufficient to go around, although at the time of ordering, the number seemed excessive. No chances were taken this year. The total shipped in September was fully 50 percent in excess of the number of Americans reported held by Germany at that time, and much more than sufficient to cover those captured since September.

Similarly, all preparations were made insofar as they could be by the International Committee of the Red Cross and the American Red Cross—to get the packages in time to all camps and hospitals in Germany housing American prisoners. They were shipped, along with large quantities of standard food packages and other supplies, on Red Cross vessels from Philadelphia to Goteborg, Sweden, and thence transshipped on Swedish vessels to a north German port fairly close to the camps where the largest numbers of Americans

are now held. The aim, of course, was to avoid railroad transport in Germany as much as possible.

Much thought was given to planning the 1944 package—the basis of it being "turkey and the fixins." A complete list of the contents follows:

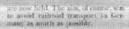

Plum pudding	⅓ lb.
Turkey, boned meat	¾ lb.
Small sausages	⅓ lb.
Strawberry jam	6 oz.
Candy, assorted	¾ lb.
Deviled ham	3 oz.
Cheddar cheese	¼ lb.

Nuts, mixed	⅛ lb.
Bouillon cubes	12
Fruit bars	2
Butter	11 oz.
Cherries, canned	8 oz.
Playing cards	1 pack
Chewing gum	1 pkg.
Butter	1⅝ oz.
Games, assorted	1 box
Cigarettes	5 pkgs.
Smoking tobacco	1 pkg.
Pipe	1
Tea	1¾ oz.
Honey	6 oz.
Washcloth	1
Pictures (American scenes)	2

The packages were paid for by the United States government, and the contents in large part were purchased through the Department of Agriculture.

Left unsaid, but implicit in every package, were the heartfelt wishes of the American people for the safe and speedy return of their kinsfolk.

Unfortunately, it was not possible to get a special Christmas package to American prisoners held by Japan, but it is to be hoped currently that the large shipments of relief supplies held in Vladivostok, which was picked up by the Japanese steamer Hakusan Maru early in November, will reach the camps in time for distribution at Christmas, just as the Gripsholm supplies shipped to the Far East in the fall of 1943 reached the men in most of the camps by Christmas.

Contents of the 1944 Christmas package for American prisoners of war and civilian internees in Europe. More than 75,000 of these packages were shipped from Philadelphia.

Chapter XIV

1944: How Long Can We Last?

Happy New Year. Whether your glass is half-empty or half-full, it *is* a new year. Coming four days after his second birthday, it is Billy Carroll's third observance—the first while fleeing Iloilo to the jungle, the second as an internee at the Iloilo City Internment Camp, and now his third at STIC. As parents of two-year-old children know only too well, the "Terrible Twos" can be challenging. What *will* the challenges in this new year be for Isabel and Norwood?

"No" is a two-year old's favorite word, but it was all too soon the favorite word of Japanese management of STIC. A prodigious change occurred for all those thousands of souls behind the sawali walls in 1944. Camp supervision changed from Japanese *civilian* authority to *military* authority, and the internees were no longer considered civilian internees under Japanese protection—they were war prisoners. STIC was now officially under the direct supervision of the War Prisoners Department headed by General Morimoto, and treatment was about to change.

The Japanese military police, the Kempeitai, were initially responsible for bringing enemy aliens into the camp, and they administered the camp for a little more than a month until February 15, 1942. After that date, the camp was administered by various civilian commandants from the diplomatic corp. Apparently, the Nipponese, as occupiers, tended to use their own civilians who were part of any captured population in administrative positions. A commandant in Baguio, for example, ran a small enterprise before the war and knew many of the internees. That had to be surreal for those incarcerated. As mentioned in chapter eight, STIC's first Commandant in 1942 was Hitoshi Tomoyasa of the Japanese military police. He was followed by the less severe R. Tsurumi of the Japanese Consular Service. On September 1st, S. Kuroda, a steel and hardware merchant from Shanghai, took over with a much harsher and ruthless hand. As luck would have it, the Carrolls entered STIC while under the authority of S. Kuroda and endured under his punitive command until October of 1943. Several other civilian commandants served until the military took over in February 1944. Now under military domination, the internees had a rapid succession of leaders for a few months until Lt. Col. Hayashi took control with Lt. Abiko as his underling. Hayashi and Abiko were inhumane and cruel. They were described as slovenly, pitiless, and vile. Norwood's original description of their new camp as a *prison* was now accurate and being war prisoners was altogether different than being held "in protective custody" as originally stated by kindly Nipponese.

A reversal of the Imperial Army's fortunes in the Pacific brought a new and merciless camp regime. Everyone was warned to show better respect for the Japanese. If a soldier or officer approached, the prisoner had to stop and bow—the upper body parallel to the ground, feet together and arms pressed tightly against the legs. This ritual was not new—it had been the norm from the beginning—but now it was far more pronounced and unpleasantly enforced. If someone failed to bow "correctly" to a guard during the day, a vicious slap to the face or a thrust from a rifle butt was applied. Older internees had obvious difficulty with the new enforcement, having to rise and bow if resting on the lawn. Bowing also took a ridiculous amount of time. When asked what he did all day as internee/prisoner, Norwood replied that, along with required gardening and supervised daily chores, *hours* were wasted standing in line for chow and bowing to the guards twice a day at roll call.

Trepidation grew with the takeover by the War Prisoners Department. Several internees who had served time in Fort Santiago, Manila's principal military prison, knew firsthand how the Imperial Army treated its prisoners.

MacArthur had used Fort Santiago as a headquarters, but after the occupation it served as the military control center for the Kempeitai, its primary use being an interrogation and torture hot bed. Reports of merciless Japanese brutality and cruelty terrified the STIC population, and the stories were indeed terrifying—a whole different and horrible story. Was their new distinction as "prisoners" going to mean they would suffer the same abuse?

Complete severance of outside communication was the military's first objective. The Package Line was closed, and no forays into Manila were allowed. Those in Manila's hospitals were brought into camp, and no outside doctors or nurses were allowed in to help. This put a terrible burden on the camp physicians. Outside news was halted, even that ridiculously edited Manila Tribune. Long lacking in "news," the last edition permitted inside carried a few last reports that, according the Elizabeth Vaughn, were quite entertaining:

> Americans have long noses to heat air as it is drawn in in a cold climate.
> Americans are tall because they have tall legs.

Before the military changeover, toward the end of 1943, the Executive Committee, now headed by Carroll C. Grinnell, the President of the General Electric Company in the Philippines, sensed that a period of extreme privation was about to begin. Secretly, the committee began amassing food in the camp warehouses (*Carroll C. Grinnell—no relation to Earl Carroll who first held the chairmanship, nor Norwood Carroll—was elected to the Executive Committee and appointed chairman by the Commandant midway through 1942).* Fortunately, some staples were acquired right before the prices soared or before they vanished entirely because when the food supply was usurped on February 1, the internees' ability to stockpile against any future shortages was gone. Outrageously long and time consuming before February, the chow lines were now nearly unbearable, and the food unspeakably worse than anyone could have feared. Everyone in the camp was now "on the line"; there were no more hearty meat stews for the wealthy. Rations were cut time and time again, and this was just the beginning. Intriguingly, knowing that protein was a vital nutrient, large quantities of a small fish, the *sap-sap,* were provided once a week by the Japanese but the quality and freshness were questionable and sometimes even completely spoiled. The cleaning of these tiny ocean fish was beyond exasperating. Usually, just thrown in the soup vats whole, the resulting incredibly noxious odor revolted the internees, until hunger took over.

157

By mid-February, the Japanese authorities went even further in their directives and overturned the entire elaborate governmental structure of the Executive Committee. Reorganizing the whole organization into four departments, they appointed their own internee representatives, but retained Grinnell as their main liaison to the camp populace.

As much as the changeover foreshadowed misery and gloom, there were a few unexpected surprises. Life in the shanties, as depicted in chapter ten, saw a big change in February. Families were now allowed to live together all the time, not just during the day. This concession seems curious when all other rules were becoming so rigid. Perhaps the Japanese finally saw the obvious easing of the overcrowded living. The guards, fully able to see inside the shanties, were now ordered while patrolling to avert their eyes if anyone was dressing, but for the most part they peered into the shanties day and night and staged surprise but ineffective searches for the clandestine camp radios. A rather bewildering surprise befell the camp when a large shipment of fresh eggs and bread arrived—neither, of course, having been available for months earlier. The reasoning for such largesse was baffling but welcome. Those food shipments happened several more times.

The women, many heretofore spoiled and pampered by the luxuries of domestic help, were pretty helpless in the matter of food preparation when first interned. Remember, they were told upon arrival to the Philippines that cooking in such a climate would be *fatal* to a white woman. The reality of camp life quickly and harshly set in, but resourceful women do what resourceful women do: make something out of nothing. And as 1944 wore on, that is exactly what they did.

Since the principle food was either cornmeal mush or a watery rice mush called lugao (salt being the only additive), the women got particularly creative. Already they had devised ways to make flour out of rice, corn and cassava. Stalks from bananas, peelings from vegetables, hooves from carabaos—these and many other items were boiled to make broth. Oil and sugar were gone, so facial cream was sometimes used as fat for frying. Fruits and vegetables were disappearing, and items from the Christmas Red Cross relief packages that were squirreled away by the cautious few were dwindling. Pigeons, rats, dogs and cats were vanishing. From Frederic Stevens book, *Santo Tomás Internment Camp:*

One lady who wishes to remain anonymous gave a recipe for preparing curried cat. According to her it tasted much like rabbit. After the cat was skinned and cut into small

159

pieces, it was dropped into boiling salt water and boiled until tender. This sometimes took several hours if one were cooking a mangy old tom cat. While the boiling was going on, a curry sauce was mixed with garlic and simmered till thick. When the meat was tender, it was dropped into the sauce and cooked slowly until they forgot what it was. Several families had this delectable dish for their Thanksgiving dinner in 1944.

The people who ate dogs tried to get the puppies. These were skinned and cut up into small pieces and boiled until tender. Then a gravy was made of rice flour and the meat added and cooked. This was served over roasted rice.

It is hard to imagine eating puppies and cats, but starvation begets desperation. Weeds and leaves from hibiscus bushes and trees that were first dried and used to make cigarettes were now stewed or chopped and eaten as salad. Food poisoning resulted from trying to eat hemp and various roots or bulbs. Roasted ground rice husks served as a coffee substitute as there were three cups of coffee per person during the entire month of June.

Food, food, food! It was an intense longing for the starving internees, and for the Carrolls, it was an overwhelming and pressing challenge. Isabel recounted in the Raleigh News and Observer:

Food was an obsession with us. We thought of it, talked of it, dreamed of it constantly. All of the women would sit long hours discussing preparation of favorite dishes, and even the old men would swap recipes. Always we were hungry; always there were gnawing pains in our stomachs. We had to stop the children from running and playing because they needed to conserve what strength they had.

This obsession ran wild throughout the entire camp—a desire that couldn't be met—and the energy it took to fawn and drool over the pictures of glorious food was stimulation that the ravenous souls could ill afford. Also, from Stevens' book are the following poems penned by two internees that illustrate that all-encompassing addiction with food. It is amazing that any humor could endure.

> I don't know why, but when I've et
> This lugao, I feel hungry yet.
> When I get out, I'm going to buy
> The biggest steak my wife can fry.
> And then I'll say "Ma'am if you please,
> Some pickles, and onions and limburger cheese."
> I'll buy new teeth to masculate,
> And I'll eat it all and lick the plate.
> > J.E. McCall

> Oh, little onions in a row
> I wish to hell that you would grow.
> Sometimes I half believe that you
> Are waiting for MacArthur, too.
> > Marie Wagner Janda

With the diminution of needed nourishment, people, of course, lost weight. Most women weighed less than 100 pounds, and the men were dropping 40-70 pounds. Doctors pointed out to the Commandant that a steady loss of weight, week by week, had commenced with the relentlessly diminishing diet. "Au contraire," replied the Commandant. "Weight loss is due to worry. Separation from home and families and the worries that accompany internment are the major cause of such a condition—not insufficient food provided by the Japanese—so try to enjoy your internment and play sports, have boxing matches, take dance classes." Of course, the Executive Committee recommended those activities be curtailed. The energy expended on them was far too great. Daily room cleaning, laundry, camp chores and gardening were difficult enough. And to add hardship to the dwindling energies, the Commandant ordered a new bamboo fence be built within the camp walls in addition to installing barbed wire on the existing fence. The internees were furious and refused, citing the Geneva Convention laws against forced labor of enemy civilians, but the Commandant replied that the convention laws had no application to Santo Tomás. STIC was being run by the sovereign rules and regulations of the Imperial Japanese Army.

When asked for verification, no proof of such regulations was produced, but two sets of stern written demands from Lt. Hayashi followed a second day of the internees' refusal to work. Under considerable protest, the camp leaders finally signed off on the orders.

As daily existence grew increasingly bleak, the creative and much appreciated entertainment produced by Dave Harvey was even more of an important part of the internees' lives—it helped to distract them from their hunger. As difficult as it was to continue his skillful productions, Harvey knew he couldn't quit. But a catchy little song that was sung at a comedy minstrel show in late June offended the guards, so the humorless Commandant requested copies of the song's words and a written apology by the four men who sang it. When asked why they must apologize, the men were told the song criticized the food in camp. *No one* was to criticize the camp in any way, and the penalty for singing the song was termination of all shows on the plaza. The Commandant did allow movies and recorded musical offerings, but that was all. One internee, according to Frederic Stevens, compared camp life to a strip tease—little by little things were being taken away.

On the 21st of September, a day like any other during this abysmal year of want, a thrilling thing occurred.

According to Norwood, "The sky filled with those American Eagles swooping down to drop their eggs on the little sacred sons of Nippon." As a preamble to this day during the previous week, bombs could be heard falling in the distance, and it gave the internees a rush of hope and joy. But on the 21st the cloud-dotted blue sky blackened with carrier-based Vought F4U Corsairs blitzing Manila. Those beautiful planes with big stars under their bent wings instead of the hated Zeros with red dots sent chills down the spine of every internee. From Tessa Cates *Drainpipe Diary:*

There were so many bombers that it was impossible to count them as they flashed rapidly across the sky. A large Japanese transport plane had tried to reach safety, but our bombers literally blew it from the sky. Like bits of burned paper carried by a high wind, we saw the plane fall and drop. We pounded each other until we were black and blue, and we shouted until we were hoarse. We behaved like pagan Romans watching the lions devour the Christian martyrs.

They came again at 6 p.m. This time, our bombers came in waves of thirty-six. Enemy aircraft popped furiously, but thank God, their many weeks of practicing hadn't helped their aim. Our audacious bombers circled, dipped, swooped, dived and dropped their bombs, thumbing their noses at the enemy aircraft.

Peter Wygle in *Surviving a Japanese P.O.W. Camp* described it as follows:

There was no pattern bombing from altitude. The pilots seemed to know exactly what they were after, and they went after it with a vengeance. The dogfights were interesting to watch, because the Jap Zeros were so much more maneuverable (but they seemed to be quite a bit slower) than our Corsairs. The Zeros looked like they were turning square corners, and the Corsairs would mush around after them, but our people seemed to get every plane they went after sooner or later.

Many internees wept as they saw those first planes. Aerial acrobatics, the dull thud of bombs, the shells whizzing through the air—those sights and sounds thrilled each and every man, woman and child. As they were herded inside with antiaircraft shells falling everywhere, it was a mad dash to the windows, keeping a wary eye out for guards who threatened to shoot them if caught gawking. Norwood allowed that you could read a newspaper that night by the light from the fires in Manila Bay, and sleep was surely elusive to all.

Reveille the next morning, screeching over the loudspeaker, was Bing Crosby warbling "Pennies from Heaven." The wake-up committee must have loved their job as there was often a humorous ditty to rouse the camp as war news filtered in. A few days after the initial air raid "Lover Come Back to Me!" awakened everyone with the hope of another visit from the daring bombers. "Ding Dong! The Witch is Dead" roused the camp when Hitler was rumored to have been killed in Germany, and "It's Three O'Clock in the Morning" rang out when the bombing of Davao southeast of Manila was whispered to have occurred at 3:00 A.M. Later, in November the crew, longing wishfully for an early Japanese retreat, played "Why Don't You Get Out of Town?" Lt. Hayashi was clearly annoyed. He unsurprisingly ordered that only wordless records could henceforth be played, and then only a few days later banned the playing of recorded music entirely. Strip teeeeze.

This initial raid and subsequent forays—"air raid ya dope, air raid ya dope!"— were the reason little Billy Carroll was "whirly dervishing" about as a toddler. The raids continued off and on throughout October, and Lt. Hayashi angrily vowed that if anyone was caught scanning the skies they would have to stand in the blazing sun and stare at that sky for *eight* hours. And some unfortunates did.

From the book *History of World War II* by Francis T. Miller:

On October 20, electrifying news was passed person to person at Santo Tomás: Allied forces under General MacArthur had landed at Leyte, surprising the Japanese. The news reached the camp over the internees' clandestine radio and was confirmed by Filipino guerilla radio broadcasts outside the camp. (*The guerillas went to some trouble for this broadcast. One secret broadcasting tower was powered by men riding bicycles hooked to an electric generator.*) MacArthur stood on the bed of a broken-down Signal Corps truck on a muddy beach at Leyte in a drenching tropical rainstorm and broadcast to the secret radio network:

This is the voice of freedom. General MacArthur speaking. People of the Philippines: I have returned! By the grace of Almighty God, our forces stand again on Philippine soil—the soil consecrated in the blood of our two peoples.... Rally to me. Let the indomitable spirit of Bataan and Corregidor lead on. As the lines of battle roll forward to bring you within the zone of operations, rise and strike! Strike at every favorable opportunity! For your homes and hearths, strike! For future generations of your sons and daughters, strike! In the name of the sacred dead, strike!

This landing at Leyte, roughly 350 miles southeast of Manila, followed by the Battle of Leyte Gulf from October 23rd through the 26th, was the beginning of the Allied takeover of the Philippines. Some 100,000 American soldiers landed along the 18-mile coast, and although the island was easily approachable by sea, a steep mountain range running north to south made gaining a foothold difficult. It took 60 days to wrest Leyte from the Japanese. This battle, often called the Battles of Leyte Gulf as there were four separate engagements, was the largest naval battle in modern history and the first to suffer the gruesome assaults of the Kamikaze Corps. The kamikazi pilots flew Mitsubishi A6M Zero planes carrying 550-pound bombs with the order to crash-dive into the American ships. Young pilots volunteered in numbers two to three times more than available planes, voicing gratitude for the privilege of dying like a man to honor the Emperor. The number of soldiers involved and the tonnage of ships destroyed was enormous. The Allies lost 2,800 soldiers, 200 planes and 37,000 tons of shipping vessels while the Japanese lost over 12,000 troops and *300,000* tons of ships. It was a massive defeat for the Japanese Empire, so gravely crippling the Imperial Navy that it never was able to engage in a naval battle with a comparable force for the duration of WWII.

The plan for this Philippine invasion was MacArthur's hard-fought-for strategy. He, as Supreme Commander of the Southwest Pacific Area, and Naval Admiral Chester Nimitz, Commander in Chief, U.S. Pacific Fleet and Pacific Ocean Areas, initially had opposing plans. Nimitz's proposal centered on the invasion of Formosa (Taiwan) which could give the Allied forces control of the sea routes between Japan and Southern Asia. It would also cut Japan's supply lines to South East Asia. MacArthur, however, stressed the moral obligation of U.S. to liberate the Philippines. Leaving the country in the hands of the

Japanese would be a blow to American prestige. Furthermore, he argued that the Philippines was a vital source of oil for Japan, and the air force they had accumulated in country could deliver a serious threat to the Allied Forces. It was a contentious dispute. Nimitz had the ships, but MacArthur had the boots on the ground. President Roosevelt, after a meeting with the two in July 1944, decided to go with MacArthur's plan. There is *absolutely* no doubt that the Carrolls and roughly 14,000 American prisoners on Luzon, not to even mention the Philippine people, were thankful that he did.

This initial Allied victory at Leyte gave the starving internees tremendous hope and optimism in their hearts, but salvation was not quite yet on their doorstep. There was more misery to endure

Marine Corsair

Japanese Zero

Aircraft carrier USS Princeton in Leyte Gulf before and after
kamikaze attack

MacArthur landing at Leyte Gulf on October 20, 1944

U.S. Landing Ship Tanks (LSTs) and troops at Leyte Gulf

FILIPINOS!

American Planes Are Bombing And Strafing This Area

REMEMBER:- We don't want to hurt you, BUT

Bombs Cannot Tell Friend From Foe!

Stay away from all military targets:—
Buildings, supply dumps, bridges and
all installations used by the Japs.

KEEP OFF THE ROADS!

By doing this you will help us to
smash the Japs and end the war

Flyers dropped on Manila to alert the citizenry

Chapter XV

Starvation: Can It Get Any Worse?

By November, STIC was truly suffering. Loss of weight continued catastrophically. The hospital reported 100-150 new cases of dietary deficiency a week, with beriberi, scurvy, pellagra—the awful diseases of malnutrition—continuing to escalate. Fillings were falling out of teeth, hair was coming out in tufts, nails were getting brittle, skin was peeling away, legs, torsos and faces were swelling, deafness, blindness, stumbling and falling were worsening—all of this was happening if one managed to still be alive. The death rate increased to a level four times greater than the previous two years of internment. From September to December 43 people died, an average of one to two every two days. A diary by Albert Holland, the head of the STIC Release Committee, was found online with the following introduction by his wife Eva J. Engel Holland. It paints a vivid picture of conditions in camp during November and December, chronicling what nearly everyone was experiencing. It is copied in part.

The diary that follows describes the plight of prisoners of STIC. It was written in the spirit of Captain Robert F. Scott:

175

"Where ultimate survival is unlikely, at least there should be an account of how the challenge was met." Or, as Albert wrote in early December 1944, "They [the Japanese] may break my health, but they cannot break my morale. Good humor is the finest mark of courage. There is one thing we have that the Japanese have not: Hope – I would rather have 950 calories a day and hope than 3000 calories and despair." Eva Holland

Nov. 18th When the Committee saw the Commandant about an increased ration, he told them "You do not realize that Japan is fighting a total war – America and England are not. Every man, woman and child in Japan is fighting the war for our very existence –**We do not care, therefore, whether you live or die.**"

Nov 21st As for food, the situation grows worse with every day.
1) The camp is out of money. This means no more coconut milk, no more watery vegetable gravies. Even though the milk and the gravies are so watery that they contribute very few calories, they help us get the corn & rice down.
2) The few cans of powdered milk the camp has left must be saved for the babies expected between now and February. It is a crime to have a baby now. Some of the parents I am sure have planned it, so there will be no delivery costs. The camp and later the Red Cross will take care of the feeding, etc. Of course, some of the babies are out of wedlock, which surely was not planned.
3) A supply of cassava root arrived – Lt. Shiragi asked for a crew to grind it into flour. Earl Carroll asked how much the

camp should be given – Shiragi answered "The camp? Well, maybe a little bit." He's absolutely shameless!

4) So, we'll need good humor. I weigh 107 now, down 11 pounds in 21 days. It is hard to climb stairs. But while I often wonder when the troops are coming, I would not want them to start until they could go forward with little loss of life. We are not important enough to waste the lives of strong young men.

Nov. 23rd Thanksgiving menu – 1 scoop rice, 4 oz thin vegetable gravy, 1 oz radish tops.   Oh, how I shall enjoy mother's dinners again!!

Nov 30th Tomorrow we go into December, our 36th month of internment. What is the situation compared with Nov. 1st? To begin with, the food is less. In calories: 950 against 1250. Camp reserves are gone. There is no more coconut milk— individual reserves are depleted. Probably not more that 10% of the internees have more than a few cans left. The health of the camp is much worse. The aged are becoming increasingly helpless – the children are growing paler, and the group from 18-50 have lost much weight. We are now forced to turn the entire gymnasium into a hospital (250 beds). Over 12% of the entire population hospitalized, and almost 15% of the adult population in bed.

From the military viewpoint our position has improved. We have tightened our grip on Leyte and Samar and have smashed all Jap attempts at reinforcement. Summing up~ If both the Marines and the relief supplies arrive in the next weeks, we'll be weak but alive. If the relief supplies arrive, the Marines can wait until Feb. If the Marines arrive, they'll have to feed us slowly back to a decent standard. If neither Marines nor kits arrive, there will be many deaths and widespread permanent physical impairment. So, Come on you Leathernecks!

The Japanese in charge of us, Lt. Kamatsu, Lt. Takeda, Lt. Abiko must have been picked from the very scum of the Army -ill mannered, boorish, cruel -disgusting in speech and appearance. It is reliably reported that a few days ago, Kamatsu refused to allow into camp a truck which was loaded with beans, eggs, milk, fruit for the children and the sick. The supplies had been purchased by neutrals outside. It cost the Japanese nothing—this is sheer cruelty and meanness. They intend to starve us. If this goes on, they'll succeed. No matter how strong the spirit, the body is becoming weaker all the time.

I weigh 99 lbs now. It is impossible to stop this steady loss of weight, but at least the rate of decrease has fallen off from 1/2 lb. per day in November to 1/4 lb. a day in the 1st half of December. Mentally I still feel very fine indeed, but I cannot stand in line, or pick up anything heavy. Sometimes my thoughts float vaguely between the desire of rest and the desire of life. Tonight, even with release nearer, I feel completely neutral, as if it makes no difference. But that is physical exhaustion.

Dec. 20th Red Cross Kit rumors stronger. The Japanese cut our rice ration today down to 200 grams net per adult, 100 grams net per child under 10-caloric content about 650 calories. This is a 25% reduction in our net rice ration. Since September the cut has been from 400 grams to 180, 55%. I weigh 97 now, and unless the relief kits or the soldiers come soon, I very much doubt that my physical strength will hold out. Mentally, I am hopeful, and far more alert than ever before. My spirits on the whole are high, but there is a physical limit to ebbing strength. My reason cannot overlook this. The thought of death is not one to revel in, but it is a possibility (indeed, in my case, close to a probability), which must be faced - coldly, grimly - I would say disdainfully. I am sure that life still has much happiness which I have not yet experienced. But many times, I have been very happy – perhaps more than I deserved. I have no complaints, I am not afraid. What Caesar says is true: Death, a necessary thing, will come when it will come. We are really just about on our last legs from starvation. The camp looks like a group of ghosts.

Dec. 23rd Two very exciting happenings today, one wonderful, one very unfortunate. Let's take the wonderful first. This morning about 10:15 18 4-engined bombers and 40 fighters passed over the camp. How very routine that sounds – but it was the most glorious sight I have ever witnessed. The B-24's or B-29's (they are not Flying Fortresses) sailed along at 15-20,000 ft - serenely, placidly, majestically. It was like seeing the Queen Mary, the Normandie, the Queen Elizabeth, the Bremen and the Europa steaming in formation in a calm sea. This is the first time 4-engined bombers have been over Manila- A good sign.

Dec. 24th This afternoon about 15 Jap M.P.'s came into camp and tore the place apart. Grinnell, the head of the camp and Duggleby, one of the camp's leaders were thrown into jail. No one knows why, but I have my suspicions and they center around getting news outside as to the terrible conditions which prevail here. And they are terrible. Tomorrow is Xmas – At once the best (hope) and the worst (physical condition) we have had. From now on it will be a race between the army and death. And, as has been written in many diaries of shipwrecked and lost souls, "God help us All."

"Terrible conditions" barely describe the reality. Energy levels were so dangerously low that school had to be discontinued. Teachers and students were far too hungry and weak to concentrate. It was during these shocking reductions of food rations that many families had to decide how to manage their meal portions. Conversations arose as to the prospects of survival and who might best be suited to care for the children, a wrenching decision that had to be faced. The women were naturally determined to be the obvious caregivers, so the fathers, unflinchingly and heroically, gave most of their meager meals to the children and mothers—growing weaker and sicker each week. It was never divulged to the Carroll family members, but Norwood surely did that very thing. As mentioned earlier, many men lost 50-70 pounds during internment, and Norwood was right in that category. Continuing his chores and gardening required huge effort, and he was wasting away. From Emily Van Sickle in *The Iron Gates of Santo Tomás:*

There were hundreds of men and women whose flesh was drawn taut over ribs and backbone, resembling the hide of starved dogs. Knees, knuckles, elbows protruded in gnarled and swollen knots, while weakened muscles stood out like cords with the slightest movement. Arms and leg bones were scarcely hidden by their parchment-thin covering of skin. And the children—it made one's heart ache to see the skinny limbs and pot bellies that resulted from an inadequate diet.

Men fared far worse than the women and fathers more than single men. Studies show that women are more likely to survive famine and disease epidemics due to biological underpinnings, and while this may have been a factor in the death statistics at STIC *(more men than women died)* it remains that the men outnumbered women in the camp, thus naturally skewing the final tally. Incredibly though, many the women—very thin and often quite ill— still tried, courageously, to keep up appearances with a hibiscus flower in their clean hair, rouge and lipstick. Possibly this display of pluck fortified those who had given up hope that help would arrive in time.

But things just kept getting worse. On December 23rd, rice rations were cut to three tablespoons per person per day, so people were eating just about anything that could be chewed and swallowed. Boiled red ants were sprinkled on the lagao by some, and the worms and insects in the dirty swept-off-the-floor rice were no longer discarded. Norwood said that the beautiful acacia, palm and native trees, if still standing—so many had been cut down for cooking fuel—were completely denuded of leaves and bark and stood like matchsticks. Granted, most of the bark was used for fuel, but some tried to boil and eat it—a terribly bitter failure. Food from the 1943 Red Cross relief kits was still being hoarded by wise cynics, fearing more months of famine to endure. Just trying to imagine the mental anguish suffered by these people—let alone the physical distress—is profoundly difficult.

In Albert Holland's diary, he mentions seeing B-24s or B-29s flying over the camp on December 23rd. These planes were not carrier planes. They were four-engined aircraft that had to take off from a land-based airfield, further indication that American troops were getting closer. Peter Wygle describes the thrill in his book:

The camp as a whole received one of the greatest presents we could possibly have been given for that third Christmas. While at a party of sorts, we heard planes. We had heard lots of planes in the three months since the air raids started, but this was different somehow. Carrier planes coming in high had a noise of their own, and this wasn't it. A formation of B-24 Liberators with a lazy cover of P-38 Lightnings was passing just north of the camp! Now, that may not sound like much in the way of Christmas goodies to you, but those babies were land-based! Carrier planes can be launched from anywhere that the water is deep enough and there's enough room to get the carrier moving like a bat out of hell, but you have to own real estate to launch land-based planes. Our side now had a big landing field within striking distance of Manila. Match THAT against your pass-it-along fruitcake and Bing Crosby Christmas music sampler record.

Along with the jubilation of witnessing the Liberators flying above came the disbelief and alarm of what the Japanese guards did next. Overall, the internees were constantly bracing themselves to expect the worst under the harsh military regime, but they were unnerved when the guards, without warning, arrested C. C. Grinnell, A.F, Duggleby, C. L. Larsen and E. E. Johnson—top members of the Executive Committee—and threw them in jail. No explanation was proffered for their arrest though many people had their suspicions as mentioned in Holland's diary.

Then, from Emily Van Sickle in *The Iron Gates of Santo Tomás:*

...a group of absurdly disguised Japanese shuffled into Santo Tomás. In a different setting, one might have mistaken them for a band of strolling, third-rate comedians; here, they were instantly recognizable as members of the dreaded secret police. Their mission was no secret: They removed the prisoners from our jail and march them away to an unknown destination.

Christmas of 1944 was looking like a pretty grim affair. A party for the younger children was organized, but sadly no Santa Claus nor presents could be devised; each child received one small piece of candy. Little Billy, now three days shy of three years old, and Peggy and Lee, five and six years old, were torpidly existing day to day along with all the STIC children—seeing life through a child's singular lens.

There was, however, a spectacular message from the skies. A plane flew over the camp on Christmas Eve and dropped a message. Christmas cards on leaflets that bore a picture of the Nativity read:

"The Commander-in-Chief, the Officers and the men of the American Forces of Liberation in the Pacific wish their gallant allies, the People of the Philippines, all the blessings of Christmas and the realization of their fervent hopes for the New Year.

Christmas 1944."

Joy and utter euphoria entered the hearts of every man, woman and child when the message was found Christmas morning. Several internees who found the leaflets passed them around for everyone to read, but the guards quickly warned that anyone caught with the message would be punished severely. Warnings such as those were regularly dismissed as annoying interference. From Teresa Cates' *Drainpipe Diary:*

> One proud American mounted his leaflet in a handsome silver frame, and a long line of people stood waiting in a back corridor to get near his prize, while spotters watched either end of the long hall for snooping Japs. Many stood in line twice to reread the beautiful message.

Hope ran so high that the gnawing hunger and weakened bodies couldn't dampen the surging spirits. It was looking like *maybe* the New Year would mark the end of their misery in this wretched hell hole—perhaps it was a decent Christmas after all. And additionally, a delightful gift from the Commandant's office was presented on Christmas morning. Curfew hour was now extended from 7:00 to 8:00 P.M. with lights out at 8:00 P.M. One must wonder if that was much of a big deal since lying down was what nearly every internee was already doing to conserve energy.

On December 28th, Billy's third birthday, the Commandant found someone in possession of the Christmas message from the skies. Punishment for that person was seven days confinement to his quarters—not terribly severe—but there was also a cut in the rice allotment for the whole camp from 700 to 600 kilos per day, a cut over and above the three tablespoons of rice per person per day meted out on the 23rd. That reduction, indeed severe, afforded barely enough food for roughly *half* of the camp's population. Lt. Hayashi was seemingly hell-bent on starving his captives.

Yet one more warmhearted concession came from the Commandant's office. New Year's Eve lights out would be 8:*15* P.M. That gave the internees fifteen more minutes to see and listen to the guards and officers reveling into the dawn at their New Year's Eve party.

So, 1944, the worst year of captivity, ended ominously. No, the Red Cross Relief Kits that could have saved many lives did not arrive, and no, neither did the truckloads of food that the international Y.M.C.A. tried to deliver on both Christmas and New Year's Day. Sentries at the front gate turned the drivers away saying, "Thanks, but no thanks—there is plenty of food in camp." And two more people died that night.

THE Commander-in-Chief, the officers, and the men of the American Forces of Liberation in the Pacific wish their gallant allies, the People of the Philippines, all the blessings of Christmas, and the realization of their fervent hopes for the New Year.

Christmas, 1944

Christmas message dropped into the camp

B-24 Liberator and P-38 Lightning as described by Peter Wygle

Men at Santo Tomás in 1944

190

Chapter XVI

January 1945: MacArthur, Hurry Please

January began with a bizarre dichotomy: funeral dirges and baby showers. The death toll was now triple that of the preceding month, but as people died, babies were born. Starvation and weakness certainly make conception difficult, but nature sometimes takes a peculiarly alternate path to its normal course as it did for many couples in these final months. The lax rules of shanty living apparently weakened starvation's power, and as related earlier there were 137 women who got pregnant by September 1944. Many of these women were frantic and tried to abort their fetuses in any way they could, believing a starving mother could not possibly provide for an infant. Others, however, carried forth—some with dread—and increased STIC's population by seventy-five infants. Were these births happy occasions? Probably not for the half-starved nurses who had to tend to the mothers and babies. Understandably, with legs swollen by beriberi and bodies weakened by hunger, the nurses were resentful of the work and additional food the mothers required. But for the mothers, a new life is a miracle under any circumstances. Many of those babies were the manifestation of desperate love in a desperate time.

191

January 6th marked the beginning of STIC's fourth year, an anniversary that was deeply depressing for the starving multitude. But thankfully the American flyboys were busy all morning bombing nearby airfields and sending internee spirits sky high. Concurrently though, the Commandant ordered, for immediate examination, all records from each of the Executive Committee's four departments, and shockingly, those records along with Lt. Hayashi's own were incinerated. Much activity and confusion ensued as internees witnessed the dismantling of living quarters and the urgent packing of food, personal equipment and camp garden tools, all of which were loaded onto trucks moving out of camp. But with fiendish glee, many silently cheered as they beheld how the enemy behaves when the conquering forces are drawing near. Just how close *were* those boys?

Continuing sorties, with little interference from the Japanese, amazed the camp until a huge B-29 took a direct hit, bursting into flames. The internees grieved as they watched the pilots eject with parachutes to an unknown end, a distressing sight.

At lights out that night, a Japanese staffer announced over the loudspeaker, "Good bye and good luck!" What? This was a bit alarming inasmuch as there was nearly no food left in camp. But early the following morning Earl Carroll and four others were summoned to Lt. Hayashi's office for the entire day, and that evening at roll call a broadcast declared that the normal camp situation was unchanged. Some of the camp gardening tools were even returned. Of course, everyone now suspected the jig was almost up, but where was MacArthur?

On January 9th while the American bombers continued daily to pommel the enemy surrounding Manila, heavy naval and air bombardment of suspected Japanese defenses was taking place at Lingayen Gulf 109 miles northwest of Manila. Encountering sparse opposition as the troops started to land puzzled MacArthur at first, but then the kamikazes appeared. Damage was heavy. Twenty-four ships were sunk and sixty-seven damaged, but the initial landing of 68,000 soldiers of the U.S. 6th Army was ultimately successful, and during the next few weeks a total of 203,608 soldiers came ashore. That enormous number of troops under MacArthur's command was reported to have exceeded the number that Dwight D. Eisenhower controlled in Europe, and the Filipino guerillas were only too happy to join the throng with resolute zeal. Maybe our boys, Filipinos included, didn't have an emperor they felt a perverse need to die for, but they both had a country, blatantly attacked, that they were willing and *wanted* to fight for. Within a few days, despite the kamikazes, our forces swiftly secured the 20-mile-long beachhead and penetrated five miles inland. But further progress towards Manila was slow—an airstrip had to be built, more troops needed to land, and preparations for aerial assistance from the Marines had to be coordinated. Superb cooperation between the three fighting forces—Army, Navy and Marines—not normally working in tandem, was remarkable.

Curiously, the Japanese Supreme Commander for Operations in the Philippines, General Tomayuki Yamashita, decided not to defend Manila. He presumed, correctly, that the American plan for invasion of Luzon would resemble the Japanese plan at the beginning of the war—land at Linqayen Gulf and then strike down the Central Valley to Manila. His plan, if the kamikazes didn't stop the Americans, was to retreat to the mountains (thus the lack of opposition at the landing) and later hit them, primarily in defensive operations as they came down the valley. This essentially should have left Manila an open city, as it had been under MacArthur three years earlier. And this was *good* news for STIC. But the best laid plans are not always followed. General Yamashita gave Admiral Sanji Iwabuchi, Rear Admiral of the Japanese Imperial Navy in charge of defending Manila, strict orders to vacate Manila without engaging in combat. Yamashita wanted to conserve his forces and avoid being trapped in an urban battle with more than a million civilians. But Iwabuchi didn't honor Yamashita's plan. A demoralizing loss of his battleship Kirishima at Quadalcanal in 1942 profoundly colored his thinking. He needed to save face, and the only way he could redeem himself was to hold his position to the death against insuperable odds. Accordingly, a scorched-earth rampage began with heavy detonations, earth-shaking explosions, and incendiarism, making certain that there would be very little left of Manila when the Americans returned.

In camp, conditions were pretty much the same: continued deterioration at an alarming rate. It cannot be overstated how bad it was. Trying to stay alive was an all-consuming business. Hungry people stole food and sneaked through the chow line for a second scoopful of mush. Children as well as adults foraged in the Japanese kitchen garbage cans for anything that resembled food. The soldiers looked on and laughed. Like a cancer, hunger ate at everyone's body and mind.

A cart drawn by a man whose job it was to escort the dead from camp replaced the hearse that originally performed that function. The wooden wheels of the cart, clattering on the walkways reminded everyone that death might not be too far away, and there was nothing they could do about it.

One morning the guards killed and butchered a carabao while internees looked on. Like a horde of the living-dead, they pathetically swarmed the remains of blood, bones, entrails, dirt, hooves, horns, ears and tail to score a bit of anything they might eat. The guards loved it.

Norwood, now weighing about 90 pounds and surely suffering from beriberi, was admitted to the camp hospital, and Isabel now had to deal with Lee, Peggy and Billy by herself. Her grit and faith in God were her only companions in dealing with the fear of losing the man whom she loved and had suffered with for these three abysmal years. But her faith had to be faltering. Two and three men were dying each day. Death certificates presented to the Commandant's office were overwhelmingly characterized as death by malnutrition or death by starvation, and this infuriated the Japanese medical officer in charge of prison camps in the Philippines. He felt it unfairly impugned his oversight of the camp populations. When Dr. Stevenson, the lead doctor of STIC refused to change the certificates, he was jailed for failing to "cooperate" with the Japanese. Some internees hailed Dr. Stevenson as a martyred hero, while others, and surely Isabel, thought his failure to cooperate was a disservice to the camp. He was of no help to Norwood nor the others languishing in the camp jail.

But as Albert Holland wrote in his diary: "I may be ill, and I may not have food, but I have hope." And now, finally, *all* the skeletal captives at STIC had hope—hope that marched down the mountains to the shores at Lingayen Gulf on the January 27th in the guise of the 1st Cavalry Division, the division that MacArthur chose to rescue STIC, the division that became the major part of the storied "Flying Column." This group of men (*The company of 1st Cav soldiers that arrived at Leyte in December*) had just spent 72 days in continuous combat in the mountains against Yamashita's troops, 40 of those days enduring 35 inches of rain. They arrived at the staging point in the town of Guimba, 35 miles from the gulf, on January 30th needing a rest, but there was none to be had. The drive to Manila was leaving in two days!

But as an important aside, twenty-four hours before the 1st Cavalry drive to Manila commenced, a group of one hundred U.S. Army Rangers and Filipino guerillas made a daring raid on the POW Camp at Cabanatuan, 75 miles southeast of Lingayen Gulf, freeing 513 men who had endured not only the Bataan Death March, but three more years of starvation, arduous manual labor, and daily gratuitous thrashings. In a coordinated attack under the cover of darkness, the Rangers with Filipino support fought through twenty-five miles of Japanese lines, killing scores of the enemy, and liberated those shattered men. When MacArthur heard the report of this incredibly successful mission—knowing that Cabanatuan was on the way to Manila—he gave startling orders to Major General Verne D. Mudge, the 1st Cavalry Commander. "Go to Manila! Go around the Japs, go through the Japs, bounce off the Japs, save your men, but *get to Manila.* Free the internees at Santo Tomás."

USS Pennsylvania

Failed kamikaze attempt

USS Columbia

USS Louisville

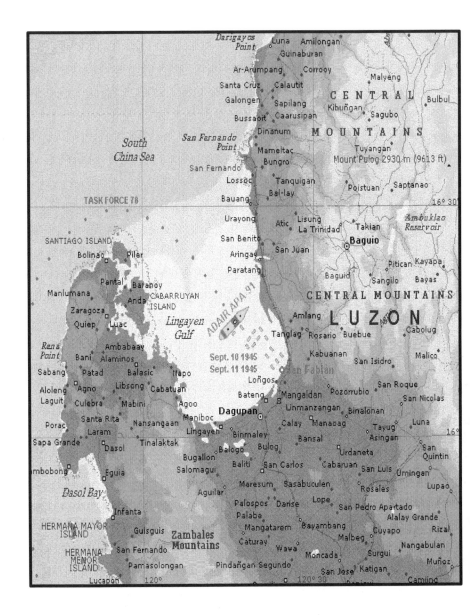

Lingayen Gulf

MacArthur coming ashore at Lingayen Gulf

Freed Bataan Death March soldiers at Cabanatuan

Chapter XVII

100 Miles to Manila in 66 Hours

MacArthur's directive to Mudge, which many believe was formulated only a few hours before it was made, ended up as one of the most audacious and gutsy actions by any military organization in American history. It was presumed that alarming intel had reached MacArthur that claimed the Japanese planned to slaughter the entire population of STIC once they knew the American approach was imminent. It was, therefore, imperative that his men get to Manila as soon as possible. "Replicate the mission at Cabanatuan—surprise the Japs at STIC!" Both MacArthur and Mudge were aware that the Army's 37th Division was only 25 miles from the capital city, but they were on foot and the motorized 1st Cavalry could move faster. Therefore, the 100-mile dash through enemy territory had to be accomplished without the usual reconnaissance, flank protection or consolidation of positions. Speed and surprise were the number one factors: avoid lengthy battles with the enemy and push through with as many men, tanks, and artillery as possible.

This particular Flying Column was MacArthur's conception. What *is* a flying column? It is a small, independent, military land unit capable of rapid mobility. It is often an ad hoc unit, formed during the course of operations. As mobility is its primary purpose, a flying column is accompanied by the minimum of equipment and generally uses suitable fast transport. Organized by Major General Mudge, the commander of the 1ˢᵗ Cavalry, and commanded by Brigadier General William Chase, this Flying Column had three brigades consisting of a total of 1,016 men from the Army, Navy and Marine Corps—by definition, not very small. At one minute past midnight on February 1ˢᵗ, carrying only four days' rations, an absolute minimum of arms, ammunition and fuel the three groups moved out in tandem on three separate roads. From sunup to sundown a nine-plane air cover of Marine SBDs (ship-born divers) flew overhead searching for roadblocks to bomb and signs of enemy movement to report. Intermittent intense fighting carried on into the night, but with the Marine SBDs protecting their left flank from Yamashita's troops scattered in the mountains, the Flying Column was able to continue its drive.

By morning on February 2ⁿᵈ the route through the town of Cabanatuan was open and the Flying Column moved steadily on, many times at speeds of 50 miles per hour. A Marine radio operator in a jeep behind the column was positioned to relay messages to the pilots, communicating reports both ways. Only a Jarhead could communicate with the Marine pilots—off limits to a GI. Master Sergeant Robert D. Holland was one of those Marines. He relates the following in his book *100 Miles to Freedom*:

Early that day (*February 2nd*) right after we were beginning to move steadily, we heard on my jeep's radio speaker: "All A-24s, THIS IS K-RATION-1. (*K-Ration-1 was Holland's call sign*). CALL OFF YOUR STRIKES AND RETURN TO BASE. REPEAT RETURN TO BASE!"

I said to the 1st Cav guy sitting with me in the jeep, "That's us—I am K-Ration 1. Who the hell was that?" I thought for a moment and knew who it was. It was a Jap on our VHF frequency. We had been warned that this might happen. I picked up my microphone and said, "Get off the air you Jap son-of-a-bitch! Pilots, pay no attention to that Jap! DO NOT RETURN TO BASE! If you hear that Jap again, ask him to say "HONOLULU!"

There *were* two incidences where the planes did return to base only to learn that the Japanese had duped them, but the march to Manila carried on. Detours around demolished bridges and skirmishes necessitating heavy artillery fire did little to curb the forward momentum. As the column rolled past, Filipinos cheered and waved, giving the boys flowers, chickens, eggs, and bananas. The soldiers had no idea what to do with raw eggs or chickens, but they loved the attention and knew it came from the Filipinos' hearts. By midnight on that busy day of February 2nd, the Flying Column was fifteen miles from Manila.

Morning sun greeted the Flying Column as it pushed on into the town of Novaliches, which the Japanese were defending at all costs. A bridge over the Tuliahan River appeared intact to the Marine aviators, but soon it was discovered to be heavily mined with four hundred pounds of TNT and thousands of pounds of picric acid (a military explosive), with the fuses already lit. Lt. (JG) James P. Sutton, a Navy bomb-disposal expert who must have had some kind of other-worldly bullet proof protection, ran onto the bridge as bullets zinged over and around him and cut the burning fuses. Regrettably, he had no time to remove the explosives. But before the Japanese returned to relight the fuse and blow up the bridge, which definitely made it difficult for the following reinforcements, the forward echelon pushed on and crossed into the Manila city limits at 6:35 p.m. It is February 3rd and the United States Army was in town.

In STIC the continued strafing and bombing by the B-24 Liberators kept hope alive with the invariable question being asked by all, "When can we eat?" But on the morning of February 3rd the planes didn't bomb or strafe. They simply flew in from the north, circled around and flew back as if performing reconnaissance, and as the sun set that evening—a dazzling spectacle of magnificent colors that only God's paintbrush could bestow—a wonderful thing happened. From Teresa Cate's *Drainpipe Diary:*

> Six of our bombers flew over the Main Building! This time they came so close that we thought they'd scrape their paint on the high tower. While screaming adults and children waved and cheered, the goggled and grinning pilots dipped their wings, and one of them threw an object in the east patio.

That object was a pair of goggles with a note attached. Norwood and Isabel always said the note's message was, "Roll out the barrel, tomorrow is Christmas Day." Other accounts all had different wording, just like a message whispered into the ear of one person is always different by the time it reaches the ear of a person down the line. But whether it said Christmas was today or tomorrow or not at all or the gang's all here, the message sent the internees into a frenzy. Five months had passed since those first Corsairs flew over camp, and in the meantime *so* many people had died waiting for their supreme hope of deliverance.

Around seven p.m. after the evening roll call and lights out, gunshots were heard. Nothing was particularly unusual about that. But the rat-a-tat-tat of machine guns in the distance started furiously popping, intensifying and then coming closer and closer. It could easily mean that the Japanese were engaging with guerillas. This happened a lot. Hope, though, sprang anew when shouts of the Filipino salutation "Mabuhay!" were heard. The suspense became utterly unbearable. Rumors and guesses flew about like startled starlings, as did the internees. Was that long overdue Santa Claus really coming? Isabel, at this moment, was at Norwood's bedside in the hospital, able to hear but unable to see the chaos. Where were Lee, Peggy and Billy? Were they asleep in the shanty or was a friend watching them for her?

The Japanese soldiers also ran helter-skelter to their posts and to two trucks that rolled out of the front gate as the furor neared the rear of the camp. In the growing darkness, the clanking of tank treads and the roar of internal combustion motors could be heard. Those tanks could be Japanese. A disturbing rumor had spread that the guards were going to murder the entire camp; they had already requested a list of males 18 to 50 years old. But they could also be American. Was it possible that they had finally arrived? It was hard to believe anything after so many

210

disappointments. Slowly the tanks rounded a corner, the way well-lit from the demolition fires Iwabuchi had created throughout the city, and the growling machines neared the front gate. The clattering noise stopped. Internees' ears at every corner of the compound were straining to hear *anything*. A flare went up lighting the darkened camp, and its glow revealed the hour on the Main Building's clock: 8:50 p.m. And then everything, again, was quiet.

Imperial Japanese Army General Tomoyuki Yamashita

Sanji Iwabuchi Rear Admiral in Japanese Navy

Marine SBD protecting the Flying Column

Chapter XVIII

Liberation at Last?

A voice rang out in the dark. "Where the hell is the front gate? Is this it? OPEN UP! Open the goddamned thing or I'll come in anyway." Oh dear God, thought those within earshot; that surely sounded colloquially American. A few gunshots and a grenade were lobbed over the fence by the Japanese in response. A jeep idling with Captain Manuel Colayco, a Filipino guerrilla leader who had met the armored brigade at the outskirts of Manila, guiding them safely through the mined streets to the university, was hit by that grenade. The brave soldier was killed, making him the first Allied casualty at STIC. With that, the "Battlin' Basic," from the 44th Tank Battalion, was waiting no longer. With engines revving mightily, the MA41 Sherman tank bolted forward and crashed through the gate with the "Georgia Peach" and "Ole Miss" following close behind.

As the tanks slowly made their way up the avenue to the Main Building, with infantry cover walking alongside and searchlights blazing, the throngs burst out of the buildings. Hysterical men, women and children, gaunt and hollow-eyed, swarmed the Plaza, sobbing, laughing, and shouting. Then suddenly, as if almost in a single voice, they

215

sang "God Bless America." Gunshots rang out as the Japanese defended their positions. Even while the shelling continued, Isabel left Norwood and dashed out of the hospital, sprinting toward the leading tank. "They tell me that she kissed every 'Joe' in the bunch," declared Norwood with a twinkle in his eye when later asked about that day. People were crawling on their stomachs in the hail of gunfire to reach the tanks. Kisses were flying as fast as the bullets. Lucy Olsen, one of Isabel's best friends, had her calf nearly blown away during those first few minutes. The scene was utter mayhem. And where were Lee, Peggy and Billy?

Soon many internees were shocked back to reality when they realized that the 1st Cavalry now inside STIC was a mere band of 800 GIs surrounded by a city held by 16,000 Japanese. From Emily Van Sickle's *The Iron Gates of Santo Tomás:*

We pressed through crowds of internees on the plaza and came suddenly face-to-face with our soldiers: twice as big as life to our starvation-ridden eyes, those husky young giants of the First Cavalry Division. Our joyful thoughts were too turbulent for articulation. We were stunned by the very suddenness of liberation, awe-stricken that so minute a force could have achieved instant victory—for our entire first-wave liberating army rode into camp in three tanks and a few jeeps.

216

This melee of crazed jubilants caused the soldiers a great deal of trouble. Unable to maneuver their tanks and engage effectively with the Japanese, the confusion gave Lt. Hayashi and sixty-three terrified Japanese guards a chance to hole up in their administrative offices in the Education Building. What the American G.I.s did not realize as they swung their tanks around, pointing their massive 75 mm guns capable of hurling a twenty pound shell up to eight miles at the building and discharging two thunderous rounds, was that 276 internees were also trapped inside that building. When apprised of that grim situation, the Americans held their fire.

Japanese guards rushed up the stairs and sealed the internees in their rooms. Only moments before, the prisoners had breathlessly watched the heaven-sent tanks approaching, relishing, at last, the thrill of deliverance. Now they had to stand silently at strict attention in hopes of not provoking the enraged guards. Barriers were placed at the stairways to prevent escape and defensive positions were secured. When one brave internee shouted out of the window to alert the troops that they were all on the third floor, blazing machine-gun fire riddled the second floor, tearing through the walls and windows and killing several guards. Retaliatory pot-shots sputtered from several

217

different windows wounding a few men standing outside the tanks. The searchlights were then extinguished. Losing no time, the Japanese ran up to the third floor and put themselves behind and amongst the internees. Once again, the guns went silent. For the rest of the night, the hostages lay on the floor under their beds and the Japanese shared their dormitory side by side. Outside the Education Building, the American troops dug in. No one slept well that night.

While intermediaries were busy trying to talk the Japanese into a surrender, the rest of the camp was getting its first taste of Army K-rations. The soldiers hate the stuff, but to the internees it was ambrosia. Relief food supplies for the camp were still 100 miles away, but all the rice and goods in Japanese storage were now released, and the parties shared what they had—even the very last cans of Spam from the 1943 Red Cross packages. Women were in awe of the strong and handsome young soldiers, and the soldiers were likewise only too happy to see the women, even though some soldiers cried when they first saw how emaciated everyone was.

Wives and mothers of the men and boys in the Education Building (there were only four women) were relieved when the guards were convinced to allow a warm lunch inside to feed them. But under scarcely concealed bitter stares, the guards ate nearly all the food before giving the hostages the scraps. All day the negotiations to surrender were futile until Lt. Col. Charles E. Brady, executive officer of the 1st Cavalry Brigade, accompanied solely by Ernest Stanley, the camp interpreter, entered the Education Building on the evening of February 4th.

Together with six armed guards, Lt. Hayashi came forth and demanded that his men be set free with their machine-guns, grenades, and individual arms to join the Japanese forces in the city. Intense and lengthy talks lasted throughout the night, and right before daybreak one of the strangest dramas of the war took place. The Japanese walked out of the Educational Building in single file, carrying their dead comrades and one rifle each, and stood at parade rest in front of the line of American tanks. The exhausted newly liberated internees as well as the rest of the camp watched as the guards and Lt. Hayashi were escorted out of STIC, some of the children yelling, "Make them bow! Make them bow!" From Bruce E. Johansen's *So Far From Home:*

The Japanese soldiers seemed nervous as they contemplated their fate in a city where their authority had collapsed. They urged the American troops to escort them all the way to Japanese lines. At Legarda and Aviles street, Lt.

219

Col. Brady told Lt. Hayashi that the escort would end. "This is where we leave you," he said. Hayashi fidgeted nervously, then saluted Brady. Brady returned the salute, as each of the 65 Japanese saluted or bowed to Brady.

Accounts differ regarding what happened to Hayashi and the guards after the Army released them. Several narratives fueled by rumors indicate that Filipino guerillas, knowing where the drop-off point was, picked them off one by one. Such accounts made the majority of internees utterly jubilant, but left many others with the realization that the vengeful punishment would not nor could not bring back those loved ones who had died so cruelly of starvation. It is only a guess as to the feelings of Isabel and Norwood, but they probably fell in with the majority. Even long after the war, Norwood could never be convinced that the Japanese were even human.

Also conflicted are versions of Ernest Stanley and his role as interpreter of STIC. To the internees, he was a reviled collaborator with the Japanese as he enjoyed separate living quarters and special treatment by the commandants. He spoke to no internee for the duration of captivity, and many thought he was a British spy. From Robert Holland's *100 Miles to Freedom:*

220

When the 1st Cavalry soldiers arrived on February 3rd, one of the American officers shouted, "Where is Mr. Stanley?" The internees immediately thought, "Now he will get his." Stanley appeared, and the officer handed him an Army steel helmet and a carbine rifle and said, "Mr. Stanley, how glad we are to see you." It turned out that Stanley had been planted in Manila and was operating as an intelligence agent for the United States, sending information outside the camp through Tobo. Tobo, a Nisei-American, had been planted in Manila as a hairdresser sixteen years before and acted as a link between Stanley and the guerrillas. It is likely that information from Stanley, passed through Tobo, had reached General MacArthur, which led to the urgency of establishing the Flying Column to release the internees of Santo Tomás.

This sounds good, but it begs the question as to how Stanley could be planted in STIC when he was simply in the Philippines as a missionary and captured unaware like everyone else in January 1942. It is possible he was a British spy, and certainly intel could have passed between Stanley and Tobo, but it seems a bit improbable that he would be an embedded intelligence agent for the U.S. when the entire Japanese occupation was a complete surprise. Perhaps Stanley didn't suffer the same miserable three years of imprisonment like everyone else, but maybe he was just fortunate enough to know the captors' language to his and the camp's benefit. His able assistance in the expulsion of the Japanese tormentors from STIC was certainly his crowning glory.

Battlin' Basic—the first tank in camp
Which soldier did Isabel kiss?

Soldiers and tanks in camp

Soldiers meeting the internees

Ernest Stanley in white shirt leading Japanese from camp

Chapter XIX

What Price Freedom?

Free at last, free at last, thank God Almighty STIC is free at last. Martin Luther King's famous benediction is probably as apt an oblation of thanks as any to describe the newly liberated internees' euphoria. The loathed, abhorrent, despicable captors were *gone.* An impromptu gathering amassed in front of the Main Building with Earl Carroll presiding. From Frederic Stevens *Santo Tomas Internment Camp:*

Carroll asked that a representative from each fighting unit please attend as an honored guest, and in front of the entire camp he said:

"During the thirty-seven months of our internment at Santo Tomás several meetings were held on this plaza to present to the Camp messages of persecution, starvation and repressions by the Japanese. Those were days of great anxiety, when the basic message at each meeting was— 'tighten up your belts.'

"Tonight our program is one of celebration— celebration of our liberty, our freedom, our release from three years of captivity—and to honor in our humble and inadequate way those gallant heroes, those fine representatives of American manhood and American ideals— the officers and men of the U.S. Army, particularly the First

227

Cavalry Division, the 37th Infantry and the 44th Tank Battalion, who so bravely fought their way through the Japanese lines to make what has been termed the most dramatic rescue in the history of warfare.

"Since the afternoon of January 4, 1942, when the first American and allied civilians entered the gates of this Camp to become prisoners of the Japanese, our hopes for liberation, our conviction that our American forces would return has never faltered. Our faith, our hopes, our convictions were realized on that glorious night of February 3. America *did* return—gloriously spearheaded by America's finest, the First Cavalry, the 37th Infantry and the 44th Tank Battalion.

"We have been inspired beyond our ability to express in words, by the race from Northern Luzon to rescue Manila and Santo Tomás. We are honored to the extent that we feel humble, because our liberation was effected by units so deeply rooted in American history.

"The First Cavalry Division—with names such as Jefferson Davis, Robert E. Lee, George A. Custer and Jonathan Wainwright inscribed in its roll of honor—and a record of achievement throughout the American continent and the Pacific for almost a century. The first Brigade of this famous division was commanded by General William Chase.

"The 37th Division—composed mostly of men from the Buckeye State—Ohio—and commanded by Major General Robert S. Beightler. Steeped in the traditions of the last world war, with a record of successive achievements in Fiji, Guadalcanal, the jungles of the Solomons, Bougainville and Norther Luzon.

"The 44th Tank Battalion—which came through with the First Cavalry on February 3rd, with its tanks, trucks and service units manned with officers, fighting men and service men bringing supplies right along with the fighting units—seventeen tanks in all on the first night in Manila to liberate and stand guard over Santo Tomás, Bilibid and Malacañang. My greatest thrill on the night of February 3rd, was when those great instruments of warfare came rolling into Camp bearing the names of Battlin' Basic, Georgia Peach, Ole Miss, Block Buster, San Anton and Crusader. They possessed the power of death blows to the enemy, but their names gave eloquent evidence to the fact that they were manned by men whose hearts throbbed with the undying spirit of America. And in one of those tanks was Lt. Robert E. Lee, descendent of one of America's greatest generals.

"The 44th Tank Battalion was under Major W.P. Meredith and Major Ragedale, with Captain Jesse L. Walters in charge of Company B, which came as a spearhead and ably assisted by Capt. J.P. Van Windle, Lt. S.J. Campbell and Lt. Robert E. Lee.

"Words cannot express our humble and sincere feelings—our hearts overflow with gratitude. We were and still are humble in the presence of the men who risked their lives that ours might be saved.

No attempt at extolling these troops would ever convey to them the sincere thanks and overflowing gratitude the people of STIC had for their deliverance. Through these daring young giants, they knew their country had not forgotten them. At the end of the speech an internee who had hidden an American flag for his entire internment at enormous and incalculable risk brought it out onto the porte-cochère. While the throng waved and cheered wildly, the glorious Stars and Stripes, unseen for more than three years, unfurled with a stunning swiftness that thrilled everyone to their core, and a rousing national anthem burst forth from every single soul. Moments later a considerable entourage rolled through the front gate, and to the delight and astonishment of everyone, General Douglas MacArthur stepped out of his car. Besieged by a grateful and emotional mob, MacArthur shed his own tears as he recognized familiar faces and skeletal cronies from pre-war days. For many, to touch him was a breathtaking reward—this man was their God.

Yes, STIC's liberation had shattered the fetters of imprisonment, but right away fresh difficulties broke the spell of elation. STIC was a solitary stronghold encircled by an enemy determined to annihilate it, and with the exodus of the guards from camp came the Nipponese offensives. Shelling and sniping in the city started when the First Cavalry arrived and began in earnest when MacArthur reached Manila, some occurring during his visit. But after he left STIC all hell broke loose. The Camp was now a military target. Day, after day, after day, the internees were tormented by Japanese shelling. It petrified them, and the horrors of past suffering faded in contrast. An old man who had served in France during WW I said, "Nobody is brave under shell fire, you just have to take it." And what else could anyone do? They just had to take it. Bombs are one thing; shelling is another horror altogether.

Those shells started hitting their mark and people started dying. The physical and nervous shock overwhelmed everyone as they saw their comrades, wives and children torn to pieces. Shanty dwellers, defenseless in their flammable straw and bamboo habitats, were naturally the least protected, and most of them ran to the Main Building for cover. But its tall tower, rising like a skyscraper above the leveled and charred surrounding city landscape, was a perfect target, and it was quickly pummeled into a death trap. Huge explosions ripped through its walls, killing and wounding many, with one account citing more than seventeen deaths and ninety serious injuries the first day. With the soldiers and Filipinos included, that count doubled. Where Isabel and the children managed to hide is a mystery. This part of their misery was never divulged. Lee remembers, however, seeing a fist-sized piece of shrapnel embedded in Norwood's bunk in the shanty. Providence and lying in a hospital bed might have been what saved him. From Frederic Stevens *Santo Tomás Internment Camp,* after a massive explosion in the Main Building:

Bedlam broke out as men went seeking for their loved ones. One man, cursing and stumbling over the debris in Room 19 kept muttering, "Where is she, where is she?" He saw a high-explosive shell hit against human flesh and then saw dust and debris mixed with human arms, legs and bodies that were twisted and torn asunder. Where there were men and women, living and breathing, now only blood, bones, and quivering flesh. "Oh Lord," mutters the old man, "not my loved one, no, Oh Lord, not her." A soldier grabbed him and hustled him away. He came back as a stretcher-bearer, still looking, still hoping.

The doctors and nurses who for three years had never stopped working, despite their own maladies and starvation throughout, were now pressed to the limits of human endurance. But jump they did into the fray to perform major operations under shocking conditions. Shells fell on every operating room they devised, and no one knew of a safe place for the many patients. Several nights they were placed on cots outside the Educational Building, and when it rained the only thing the nurses could do was cover them with more blankets. It was war at its ugliest, and the shelling continued to rain down. The G.I.s were able to knock out the gun sites little by little, but they were suffering casualties as well. In the camp's temporary graveyard were rows of newly dug graves with the remains of unfortunate men and women who had suffered the cruelty of the Japanese for so long, only to die horribly in the end. But many died with the knowledge that their flag would float over them—that America had come back. Utterly heartbreaking were the many telegrams to loved ones back home that exulted in the joyous liberation. They were now hideously old news. Many families had not heard from their imprisoned relatives for the entire three years. To rejoice in the news that they were alive, only to find out they had died so tragically, was inconceivable.

Dodging gunfire and mortars is pretty much impossible—the shells just fall from the sky—but aim was not always sure, so life, such that it was, had to go on. Through some crazy psychological mechanism the people became, almost, inured. Of course they ducked and jumped when a shell swooshed by, but the earlier paralysis was in some way diminished. Unbelievably, it was eating real food that posed almost as big a problem. Filling a starved belly with rich food—the K-Rations especially—caused agonizing cramping and debilitating diarrhea. Toilet facilities, sorely limited due to shelling and the lack of running water, existed only on the main floor of the Main

Building and became a revolting nightmare. Also an attack of diarrhea on the third floor wasn't going to wait for a trip down two flights of stairs. Under doctor's orders soldiers tried to better control the diet when food supplies finally arrived, but the candy and chocolate given freely to the children didn't help the situation. But who on earth could blame those young men? The precious children, the Carroll children among the, were little magnets for extra attention. Telling a person who has nearly starved to death to limit their intake was pointless, and even though the soldiers tried, some unfortunates actually died from the complications of the shock to their system. Imagine starving for more than a year and then dying from plentiful food. The irony is heartbreaking.

Throughout the month of February the onslaught continued, and forty-three internees died, some from mortar strikes and others from prolonged starvation. By month's end, as our troops continued to battle the murderous Nipponese outside the camp, the incessant shelling in STIC stopped. News was discovered regarding the surprising arrest and removal from camp in December of C.C. Grinnell and the three other STIC executives. They were found buried near Manila's Harrison Park, and Grinnell had been decapitated. So for reasons that some surmised but only the

234

Japanese knew, Grinnell, Duggleby, Larsen, and Johnson were cruelly murdered. At least thirty prisoners met that end during the Japanese régime, but now, at long last, the merciless and malevolent tyranny of STIC was ended. And little by little, the emaciated and diseased bodies of the prison's survivors started to heal and recover.

The unfurling of Old Glory

MacArthur near the front facing left in the hat

Children Of Japs' Santo Tomas Camp
Learn How To Shout And Laugh Again

The following story on children's life in the Santo Tomas internment camp was written by Joan Elizabeth Bennett, 10, daughter of Mr. and Mrs. Roy C. Bennett, whose father is manager of the Manila Bulletin.

By JOAN BENNETT

SANTO TOMAS, Manila, Feb. 11 (Delayed) (P)—It is hard for us 500 children of Santo Tomas to realize we are free. But we know something wonderful has happened and we now are able to shout and laugh again.

We climb all over American tanks, get hauled out from under the wheels of army trucks and tag everywhere after our good natured soldiers who pet us and feed us candy.

I was not quite eight when the war started. Mostly, I remember our house being crowded with people who were bombed out of their own homes and our attempt to have a Christmas.

Christmas Eve, 1941 we had a little party in the house around a tree for all the children of the neighborhood.

Other Christmases were not so nice. After the Japs came into Manila they came and got Daddy and took him away because he had written things in his newspaper about them that they didn't like. We had no chance to say goodbye to him.

For nearly a year and a half we never saw him. Mother, sister Helen and myself were allowed to live in a convent because mother said the Japs wanted to shadow her to see if they could find out something which would be hard on Daddy. They never got a chance.

Daddy Is Released

Our second Christmas was made glad because we had a part in sending truckloads of gifts to our soldier friends from Bataan. The generosity of the Filipinos and neutrals was wonderful and gifts reached the prison camp safely Christmas morning, 1942.

In April of the next year Daddy was released and we joined him at Santo Tomas. Most of the people who had been here didn't like the place but it was heaven to Daddy and great for us because the family could be together again.

The next big occasion was in September, 1943, when people left the camp to be repatriated home. Daddy's name was on the list but he chose to remain here.

That year was not so bad for us children. We went to school, lived in big dormitory rooms with each person's space carefully guarded and couldn't see out of the walls surrounding the camp.

But we built a little nipa (palm leaf) shanty which became "home" where a little privacy could be found and where we could grow little gardens and brighten things up. But after the Japs cut us off from outside people last December things grew worse. Food got less and less and people began to grow thin.

The people got awfully hungry and what do you think they did? They collected all the recipes they could find of good things to eat and talked about them all the time —even the children and men.

Our pet cats and dogs were very skinny but they began to disappear and the rats came back again. Rats probably would have been in the stew pots next. The people said pussy soup was quite tasty and fried garden snail tasted like chicken.

Japs Become Mean

The Japs began to get very mean, with roll calls two times a day and forcing us to bow to every soldier we saw. There was a lot of "can't do this" and plenty of "must do that."

People, even children, fainted because they didn't have enough to eat and everyone looked like a skeleton or else was all swollen because the food wasn't right. Then the Japs used often to pull surprise inspections.

But the American air raids began and the people began to get a little more hope.

Finally the Americans came in and now everything is all right although sometimes we still can't believe it. We hear lots of shooting around us but the kids don't pay much attention. We are more interested in all the good new things to eat.

Just think, today we had real butter and bread!

This report was by a ten-year-old girl!

238

Father and son hiding during shelling

Wheeling dead internees to gravesite

Burials in camp

Real food at last

Chapter XX

The Manila Massacre

While STIC suffered constant shelling, Allied troops outside the camp were in a brutal battle to drive the Japanese out of Manila. Iwabuchi, against Yamashita's orders, had been burning buildings and bridges since news arrived of MacArthur's landing at Lingayen Gulf, but the horrors and devastation started in earnest on February 3rd.

The bloodiest fighting of the Philippine campaign occurred in the streets of the city, building by building, room by room, door by door   Nipponese soldiers rampaged through the capitol, dynamiting famous churches, universities, and hospitals. Groups of Filipino citizens were rounded up and summarily executed. At Concordia College where more than 2,000 women and children had taken refuge, the Japanese chained the doors and burned it to the ground.

Piles of dead and mutilated bodies were strewn in the streets with their hands tied behind their backs. Babies were tossed in the air and bayoneted, their eyes gouged out and smeared like jelly. Groups of families hiding in their houses had gasoline poured over them and were set afire. If any were able to run out, a nest of machine guns was waiting to

243

mow them down. Four hundred women and girls from a wealthy district were rounded up and submitted to a selection board that decided which ones were the prettiest, and then twenty five of the most beautiful were taken to the Bayview Hotel where enlisted men and officers took turns raping them, some of them twelve and fourteen years old. After the filthy assaults, sometimes fifteen or twenty times on each girl, their nipples were sliced off and their bodies bayoneted from the neck down. This carnage continued unabated day after day.

During the Allied artillery bombardment of Iwabuchi's positions, thousands of civilians were killed, and thousands more were killed in the crossfire. On February 26th, after 16,000 Japanese defenders were killed, Iwabuchi committed suicide using a hand grenade. He vowed to fight to the death and he did. His body was never positively identified.

On February 27th, MacArthur strode into the Malacañan Palace, which incredibly was untouched. It was here he restored the capital to the loyal Filipino officials who had survived the battle. His remarks:

More than three years have elapsed—years of bitterness, struggle and sacrifice—since I withdrew our forces and installations from this beautiful city that, open and undefended, its churches, monuments, and cultural centers might, in accordance with the rules of warfare, be spared the violence of military ravage. The enemy would not have it so, and much that I sought to preserve has been unnecessarily destroyed by his desperate action at bay—but by these ashes he has wantonly fixed the future pattern of his own doom.... On behalf of my government I now solemnly declare, Mr. President, the full powers and responsibilities under the constitution restored to the Commonwealth whose seat is here reestablished as provided by law. Your country, thus, is again at liberty to pursue its destiny to an honored position in the family of free nations. Your capital city, cruelly punished though it be, has regained its rightful place—citadel of democracy in the East. Your indomitable—

Here his voiced wavered, and he buried his face in his hands and wept. Wiping his eyes on his sleeve, he closed, brokenly:

In humble and devout manifestation of gratitude to almighty God for bringing the decisive victory to our arms, I ask that all present rise and join me in reciting the Lord's Prayer.

Later MacArthur wrote that the victory in the Philippines, instead of a moment of victory and monumental personal acclaim, seemed only a culmination of a panorama of physical and spiritual disaster. "It had killed something inside of me to see my men die."

More than 100,000 citizens of Manila were killed— one tenth of the entire population. The devastation of the city was one of the greatest tragedies of World War II. In twenty-eight days, 70 percent of the utilities, 72 percent of the factories, 80 percent of the southern residential district, and 100 percent of the business district were razed. Once the envy of other Far Eastern cities, Manila, the Pearl of the Orient and melting pot of four cultures, was turned into complete rubble and smoldering ash. Dresden Germany was the only city suffering a worse end, but not by much.

It is miraculous that STIC didn't meet its demise during the drive to eradicate the Japanese occupiers. Every person in that camp who survived owes so much more than a debt of gratitude to the soldiers who liberated and defended them. They owe their lives.

The destruction of Manila

Citizens' hands tied and murdered
Babies bayoneted

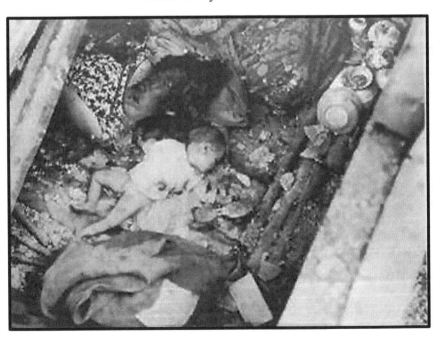

Burning of Manila

They will pay for this; for this sea of blood and flame,
For these heaps of stinking earth that once were living,
Breathing, dreaming men and women, reaching
For the stars, cut down without mercy or shame;
For these rows on rows of once-cheery homes that became
their tenants' funeral pyre; for churches lying
In the dust, shattered in an orgy of unreasoning
Destruction, all for an emperor's empty fame

They will—they must—pay for this; but not
For revenge: They knew not what they did! For them
Learning can only come the hard way:
Only when they see fall on them the shot
And shell they rained on others will they condemn
Their former ways; then will dawn a new day.

Benito Legarda, Jr.

Chapter XXI

The Long Trip Home

"When can we shake the dust from this hell hole off of our feet and go home?" No question was more fundamental than this one. Repatriation, for the organizers in the Army and the Red Cross, had to be a veritable nightmare. There were nearly 4,000 people wanting to go home while the Allies were waging the bloody battle in Manila. Logistics, to say the very least, were complex.

For the Carrolls, their new daily existence since STIC's liberation was not much different than the previous three years. Their "normal" had been waiting—waiting hours in long lines for food, waiting for the interminable roll-calls to end, waiting and praying for deliverance. But their new and not dissimilar "normal" was also waiting—waiting in long lines to register their existence with the Red Cross, waiting with everyone else for the arrangement of safe transport, and then waiting for their turn to go home. For the last fourteen years, home had been the Philippines, and the children knew no other country. Except for his first six months as an infant in the jungle, little Billy knew only captivity. For Norwood, though, the waiting was a blessing. Eating nourishing food and sleeping without constant

251

shelling was bringing him back to life and preparing him for the lengthy journey home and the difficulties moving forward.

Western Union Telegrams addressed to Margaret O'Briant, Isabel's sister in Washington D.C., started transmitting on February 22nd. The first telegram simply stated that Isabel and the children were rescued—"condition fair." The second on February 28th was from Liggett & Myers stating that Norwood was in the hospital and everyone else was safe. The third, again from Liggett & Myers, received March 2nd stated as follows:

We are pleased to advise that we are today in receipt of an airmail letter from Norwood M. Carroll dated February 15th in which he makes no reference to having been in the hospital but states that he and his wife and three children are being well taken care of by the U.S. Army and that they are being furnished the good things of life in such abundance that they are rapidly forgetting the privations and hardships of the past three years. He also states that they have asked to be returned to this country as early as possible but that the Army has thus far been unable to say anything definite as to the date of their return.

Ben Carroll Liggett and Myers Tobacco.

Choosing who could leave followed no particular order. To everyone the process was mind-numbingly arbitrary, but the personnel in charge did everything possible to make the wait bearable. Variety shows, concerts and movies were shown on the lawn every night. Astoundingly, the movie pre-show newsreels that extolled the Allied forces with real combat footage, had their own actual backdrop of red fire-lit skies and battle explosions right outside the camp. Peter Wygle commented in his book *Surviving a Japanese P.O.W. Camp;*

> I've been to the Hollywood Bowl several times for the Tchaikovsky Spectacular (1812 Overture with fireworks and cannon fire) and the effect was much the same.

No date has been found for the day Norwood and Isabel were told to pack their fifty pounds of earthly goods and be ready to depart the confines of their earthly netherworld. Part of that fifty pounds, which was the limit for all five of them, was a collection of 105 mm howitzer shells that Lee hoarded during the enemy shelling—that was not staying behind. Consensus garnered from many other internee accounts was that they were flown in a C-46 three hundred and fifty miles southeast to Tacloban, Leyte, where MacArthur had made his first assault on October 17th, 1944. To imagine their thoughts and feelings as they roared into the sky passing over their three-year prison is nearly impossible. Euphoria, worry, gratefulness, incredulity—all the above? They had survived. Their family was whole.

Surely the sight of the ravaged city, unrecognizable in any way, must have been shocking. And equally shocking was the realization that their heinously interrupted fairy-tale life was now gone forever. They now had to carry on going forward.

A tent camp had been erected in Tacloban to house the different groups while they awaited their ships, but the time spent there by the Carrolls is, again, unknown. Sometime in late March the *SS Klipfontein*, a Dutch ocean liner taken over by the War Shipping Administration in 1942, pulled into Leyte's improvised port. Everyone was awakened at midnight, given coffee and sandwiches, and ferried down to the ship. But for reasons unknown, the embarkation was delayed for eleven hours—the old hurry up and wait routine. Most of those hours were spent in stifling heat, and when it was finally learned that the cause of the delay was the slumbering commander—oh, did profane invectives erupt. Around noon, Norwood, Isabel, Lee, Peggy and Billy wearily embarked with one hundred and thirty-one passengers and finally settled into their berths. Amazingly, yet perhaps thankfully, the only thing Bill remembers from his three years in the Philippines is drinking a warm Coca-Cola from a soldier's tin cup while waiting in the broiling sun to board that ship. The sweetness of the

Coke and the hint of metal were seared somewhere in his medial temporal lobe forever. One can imagine Isabel telling little Billy to say, "Thank you," and the soldier perhaps tousling his sweaty hair.

After Major General Franklin L. Sibert was awakened, the ship set sail for Hollandia, New Guinea—a voyage of 1,500 miles. Vincent Gowen describes the trip in his book *Sunrise to Sunriset:*

At the pace we set from Leyte we seemed unlikely ever to reach New Guinea. We were travelling in convoy, some forty or fifty of us, landing craft, destroyer escorts, a freighter or two and, standing out, monumentally vulnerable, the 16,000 ton *Klipfontein.* As usual, our destination and route, officially secret, was known unofficially to everybody—Biak, Finschhafen, and thence past Guadalcanal on the long haul to San Francisco. Just ahead of us, however, as we emerged from the Leyte Gulf, was another convoy whose secret was better kept. Its four hundred ships filled the sea. Turning north, while we turned south, its foremost vessels were hull-down on the horizon before the aftermost had drawn away from us. Not till news came of the bloody assault on Okinawa did we know where they had gone.

Off Hollandia, in moonlight that made the *Klipfontein* a silver target, two torpedoes were let loose at us. Luckily, we now were traveling on our own, and turned up a burst of speed that shook us from mast-head to keel, speed sufficient to outrun any submarine. In convoy, our ship would have been a sitting duck.

While in Hollandia, the *Kilpfontein* picked up 2,000 soldiers also bound for home. The ship's holds became a bit more crowded, and the undercurrents between sex-starved Adonises and the single women were a daunting challenge to control. Suffice it to say the "controls" were futile. To boot, the homeward-bound vessel now had to ply the navy blue waters of the immense Pacific Ocean, from below the equator to above, for *6,766 miles.*

During the seemingly interminable crossing, a broadcast from Washington was transmitted on April 12th with disturbing news that President Roosevelt had died. So out of touch with American politics was everyone on board that no one, not even the soldiers, knew who his successor could possibly be. An effort to memorialize Roosevelt failed to find even one soldier who could play taps, so a scratchy recording of the Star Spangled Banner had to suffice. Grief for the President did not linger. Everyone's focus was honed on reaching American soil.

How long did the journey take? No date and time of departure from Leyte could be found, but as dawn was approaching on the morning of April 21st, 1945, the California coast came into view. Can anyone fathom the emotions that spilled forth from every person on

Klipfontein's deck? The cheering, crying, silent prayers to the heavens above had to be nothing short of a pandemonium. At long last, one hundred thirty-six prisoners of war—one hundred thirty-six thankful U.S. citizens—were about to walk down the gangplank and touch American soil. They were nearly *home.* As the ship steamed towards San Francisco Bay, the iconic Golden Gate Bridge came into view. All eyes were fixed on its breathtaking and magnificent beauty as the sun rose smack dab in the middle of it two towers. Few had ever seen this marvel of design, and those who had were just as transfixed by its grandeur. For a moment everyone was subdued—it was all so overwhelming. But as they glided under that glorious behemoth, nervously and joyously imagining what lay ahead for them, little Billy looked up at the traffic crossing overhead and whispered, "Daddy *look.* Yeeps, yeeps!

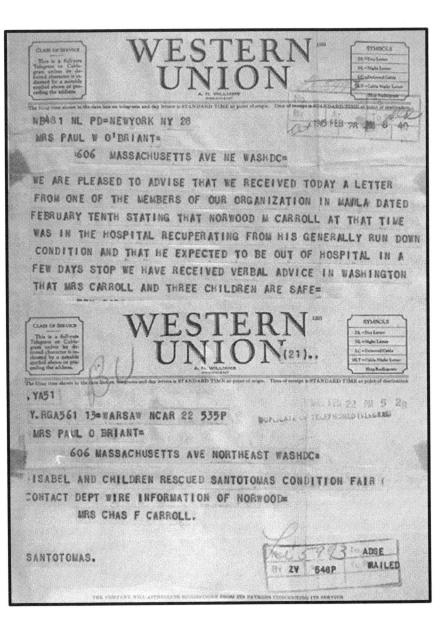

WESTERN UNION

NB461 NL PD=NEWYORK NY 28

MRS PAUL W O'BRIANT=

606 MASSACHUSETTS AVE NE WASHDC=

WE ARE PLEASED TO ADVISE THAT WE RECEIVED TODAY A LETTER
FROM ONE OF THE MEMBERS OF OUR ORGANIZATION IN MANILA DATED
FEBRUARY TENTH STATING THAT NORWOOD M CARROLL AT THAT TIME
WAS IN THE HOSPITAL RECUPERATING FROM HIS GENERALLY RUN DOWN
CONDITION AND THAT HE EXPECTED TO BE OUT OF HOSPITAL IN A
FEW DAYS STOP WE HAVE RECEIVED VERBAL ADVICE IN WASHINGTON
THAT MRS CARROLL AND THREE CHILDREN ARE SAFE=

WESTERN UNION (21)..

.YA51

Y.RGA561 13=WARSAW NCAR 22 535P

MRS PAUL O BRIANT=

606 MASSACHUSETTS AVE NORTHEAST WASHDC=

ISABEL AND CHILDREN RESCUED SANTOTOMAS CONDITION FAIR (
CONTACT DEPT WIRE INFORMATION OF NORWOOD=
MRS CHAS F CARROLL.

SANTOTOMAS.

Two telegrams dated Feb. 22 and Feb. 28 to Isabel's sister

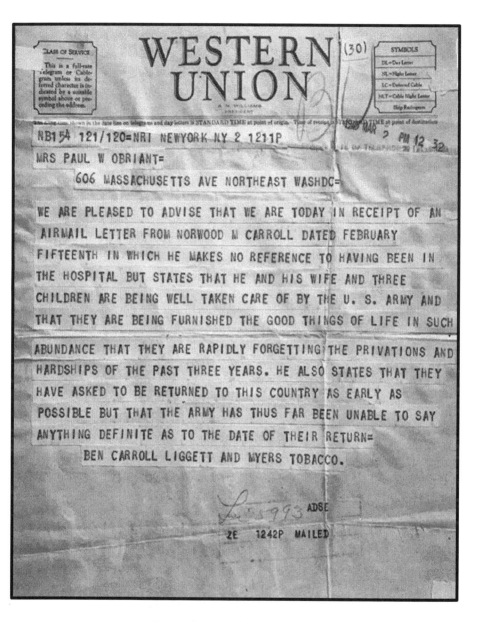

WESTERN UNION (30)

The filing time shown in the date line on telegrams and day letters is STANDARD TIME at point of origin. Time of receipt is STANDARD TIME at point of destination

NB154 121/120=NRI NEWYORK NY 2 1211P

MRS PAUL W OBRIANT=

606 MASSACHUSETTS AVE NORTHEAST WASHDC=

WE ARE PLEASED TO ADVISE THAT WE ARE TODAY IN RECEIPT OF AN
AIRMAIL LETTER FROM NORWOOD M CARROLL DATED FEBRUARY
FIFTEENTH IN WHICH HE MAKES NO REFERENCE TO HAVING BEEN IN
THE HOSPITAL BUT STATES THAT HE AND HIS WIFE AND THREE
CHILDREN ARE BEING WELL TAKEN CARE OF BY THE U. S. ARMY AND
THAT THEY ARE BEING FURNISHED THE GOOD THINGS OF LIFE IN SUCH
ABUNDANCE THAT THEY ARE RAPIDLY FORGETTING THE PRIVATIONS AND
HARDSHIPS OF THE PAST THREE YEARS. HE ALSO STATES THAT THEY
HAVE ASKED TO BE RETURNED TO THIS COUNTRY AS EARLY AS
POSSIBLE BUT THAT THE ARMY HAS THUS FAR BEEN UNABLE TO SAY
ANYTHING DEFINITE AS TO THE DATE OF THEIR RETURN=

BEN CARROLL LIGGETT AND MYERS TOBACCO.

55993 ADSE

2E 1242P MAILED

Last telegram dated March 2

259

The Klipfontein—the Dutch liner that took the Carrolls home

The Golden Gate Bridge

Chapter XXII

Lifes Goes On

It is now nearly four long months since the liberation of Santo Tomás Internment Camp on February 3rd. Little Billy and his family endured three years under the yoke of an oppressive and cruel enemy. But it is a memory that is slowly beginning to fade. They are now on their way home.

After disembarking in San Francisco, the Red Cross provided clothes and hotel rooms for the weary travelers, but nothing is known regarding the time spent there or their transcontinental trip home. Probably by train via Chicago, the Carrolls made their way to Durham, North Carolina, Isabel's hometown. Their first nights were spent at the lovely Washington Duke Hotel where, according to family lore, little Billy really liked the comfortable overstuffed wing chairs. He had never sat in anything of the sort his whole life. After joyous visits with family and many friends, the business of rebuilding a life in Durham crept in.

Billy and Peggy went to stay with their aunt Margaret, Isabel's sister, in Washington, D.C. while Norwood, Isabel and Lee stayed back to find a home and put Lee, now six years old, in school. Liggett & Myers offered Norwood the opportunity to return to the Philippines in his old position, but he declined. He knew there was not going to be much business in that country for many years, and he was ready for a more normal life in North Carolina. But staying with the company, he accepted a position as Purchasing Agent in the Durham headquarters and held it for the rest of his life.

Later when all was settled, Norwood would recall the family's horrific experience in the Philippines this way:

"Three facts stand out in my mind—the tough fiber of the American character; the innate courage of the children who suffered hunger and hardships without complaints; and the stubborn faith which sustained us through that eternity, never letting us doubt that freedom would come."

"I think that I can speak for all when I say that of the thousands of prisoners that filed out of Santo Tomás, Bilibid, Los Banos, and all the other camps, each of us feels a debt of gratitude to the men who liberated us and to the families of those who died that we might live."

Billy and Peggy came home to Durham and life returned to normal, albeit a new normal. Billy's little bowed legs that "couldn't stop a pig in a ditch" weren't bowed anymore. Proper nutrition, even after three years, performed its magic. Lee, Peggy and Billy grew and enjoyed all the things afforded to children in the '40s and 50's. They enjoyed school and played sports; Boy and Girl Scouts activities were a favorite endeavor. Each spring the children helped Norwood plant a family garden in an acre plot at a neighbor's home, a project that taught them to sow, weed and harvest the vegetables in each of their assigned rows. Eventually all three of them were enrolled at the University of North Carolina in Chapel Hill at the same time. While proud to have all his children at his revered alma mater, Norwood's favorite quip was "Yeah, it is great that all three are in Chapel Hill, but I am barely one step ahead of the sheriff." Upon graduation, Lee, Peggy and Billy went their separate ways. Lee joined the Marines and Peggy became a physical therapist. Billy—now Bill to everyone except his family and childhood friends—took a job with Cannon Mills in New York.

Ten years after the end of World War II, the world saw the beginning of another war: the War in Vietnam. And it was another ten years before its effect would be felt by the Carroll family. Lee, in Washington D.C. pursuing a business career, was no longer in the Marines, but Bill, in 1967, decided to enter the Air Force Officer Candidate School. Achieving the rank of Lieutenant, he chose to serve as an intelligence officer. An astonishing irony in Bill's service to his country was his first assigned duty station: Clark Air Force Base, Philippine Islands. When he called home to tell Norwood and Isabel how relieved he was to not be heading right away to Vietnam, there was dead silence on the other end of the phone. Recalling the horrors left behind, it must have been a bitter pill for them to have their youngest child return to that land as he had left it—in war.

Bill's first tour of duty in the Philippines was with the 405th Fighter Wing. With frequent deployments to Vietnam from Clark AFB, his time spent in the Philippines was eighteen months. Immediately following that posting, with a promotion to the rank of Captain, Bill subsequently deployed for a second one-year tour with the 7th Air Force Headquarters at Tan son Nhut Air Base near Saigon, Vietnam. While in the Philippines and Vietnam, Bill's intelligence briefings to pilots in country were of immeasurable value.

After his second tour of duty, Bill safely returned stateside. In 1969, he began a career as a stockbroker with Merrill Lynch, Pierce, Fenner, & Smith in Denver, Colorado. It was there that he met me in the summer of 1972. One year later we were married. Changes in Bill's career took us east to Virginia and North Carolina, but his restlessness for the great outdoors that he had enjoyed in Colorado sent us back west. It was the Seattle area that we ultimately chose as our home and the place to start our family. Our son Will was born in 1979, followed by our daughter Tilghman in 1981.

Life in Washington has been good, full of outdoor family adventures and plenty of hunting and fishing for Bill, his adored passions. Our home has several wonderful Philippine treasures—a hand carved chest that was in Norwood and Isabel's Iloilo home and a plein air scene painted by Fernando Armosolo, the "Rembrandt of the Philippines." The chest and various objets d'art were carefully guarded by a loyal servant in the Philippines during the war and later shipped to North Carolina. Bobby Olson gifted the painting to the Carrolls after a return trip to Manila. Bobby, cited earlier in the book, and her family were also in camp with Bill's family. They lived in Durham afterwards as well.

In 1995, Bill and I travelled to Las Vegas, Nevada to attend the 50th Anniversary of the Survivors of Santo Tomás. Bill was 53 years old. To say it was an emotional event is an understatement. Standing in line the first night to buy a drink, we started a conversation with a gentleman in his seventies who had a First Cavalry Division sticker on his name tag. The identifiable sticker, a yellow oval with a black horsehead in the center bisected by a black diagonal line, prompted Bill to remark, "I see you were in the First Cav during the war." The man replied, "Yes, I was in the first tank that crashed down the gates at Santo Tomás." Bill vigorously shook his hand and said, "Sir, I want to thank you for saving my life." He then added, "My mother probably kissed you that night," bringing a smile to both their faces. It was a moving moment to witness. Remarkably, the man hailed from Walla Walla, Washington, a mere three hours away from our home. Our chance encounter was a lovely start to an extraordinary weekend.

There were so many more wonderful and poignant moments. A call went out for anybody who was a baby during internment to come onto the stage. Five people stepped up with Bill. Turning to the man next to him Bill wisecracked, "Oh yeah, I remember you. You cried all the time in our camp nursery." It brought quite the chuckle. I witnessed another amazing incident when I saw Bill seated at a table with a handsome older gentleman wearing a dark-navy suit, white shirt and yellow tie. A crop of thick white hair heightened his striking presence (*I reference this man's appearance because he stood out from all the other attendees*). Bill asked him if he had known his father Norwood. With a serious but kind bearing the man leaned forward and said, "Norwood was your father? Son, he was a fine man—a *fine* man. It brought tears to both Bill's and my eyes.

The celebration of STIC survivors provided lasting memories for Bill and me. We both were so glad we went. But it was another twenty two years before the thought of actually going to the Philippines to see where Bill spent his first three years of life entered my mind. Our family went to Asheboro, North Carolina in 2016 to visit Bill's sister Peggy for Thanksgiving. She was not well, and we wanted to be with her. Our daughter Tilghman couldn't come because she was sharing the holiday with her new husband's family in Atlanta. But Lee, now living in Asheboro, was there for what ultimately became the last gathering of the three siblings. The evening before the family feast, Bill, Lee, Will and I sat at a table in Peggy's daughter's home discussing days gone by. The Philippines, naturally, was part of the conversation. As I listened to Bill and Lee, the proverbial light bulb went off in my head. My Christmas gift to my family was going to be a trip to the Philippines. A loving bequest from my father after his death was to make this gift a reality.

Mrs. Norwood Carroll is pictured here with her children on a recent visit to Duke, left to right, Mary Margaret (Peggy), age 5; Norwood Lee, age 6; William Singleton (Billy), age 3; and Mrs. Carroll. (Story on page 158.)

Isabel visiting Duke University with the children after their return

Carrolls Hid Out From Japs In Jungles For Six Months

FREED FROM JAPS—Shown above are the Norwood Carrolls, just returned to Durham after three years as prisoners of the Japanese. Seated are Mr. and Mrs. Carroll, with Billy, in his mother's lap. Standing in front of her father is Peggy, and standing to the right is Lee.

Lee, Peggy and Billy

Norwood and Isabel seeing Lee, Peggy and Bill off to the
University of North Carolina

Chapter XXIII

The Return 2017

General Douglas MacArthur vowed in 1942 to return to the Philippines, a promise he kept. I was determined that Bill would return as well with his family in tow. Excitement grew as Christmas drew near. A trip to the AAA travel store to find a map of the islands started the process and was the first of a number of remarkable coincidences. When I asked the woman at the entrance for an agent to help me get started, she directed me to a young woman at a nearby desk. As serendipity has its way of stealing innocently but potently into your life, it so happened that the agent was a Filipina. When I told her my idea and the reason for the trip, she queried further and learned an abbreviated version of Bill's family saga. Quite surprised she said, "The University of Santo Tomás was an internment camp? I never knew that, and I went to school there. And my father lives in Iloilo City!" I explained that my nascent plans were quite preliminary and that a map to open on Christmas morning was all I needed for now.

Plans started to take shape. Tilghman and her husband Jonathan Whitacre were coming for Christmas, so my anticipation of the Christmas surprise intensified.

Jonathan's great-grandfather, Paul Fred Whitacre, was also an internee at STIC along with his son Howard, daughter-in-law Virginia, and two granddaughters Molly and Peggy. It was an uncanny happenstance. The odds of Tilghman and Jonathan meeting, getting married, and sharing such a similar history are truly astonishing. Paul Fred died at age 58 the day of STIC's liberation and was buried on the campus. After the war, along with other non-combatants who died during internment, he was reinterred at the North Cemetery in Manila. I was determined on our journey to visit the grave.

On Christmas morning after opening all our gifts, I presented an envelope individually to Bill, Will, Tilghman and Jonathan. Inside was a map of the Philippines and a note that said:

WE ARE GOING TO THE PHILIPPINES!
It is time that we see where Bill was born and spent the first three years of his life. Next December 2017 we are going to Hawaii to visit Pearl Harbor and then journey forth to Manila. Merry Christmas.

Waiting a whole year was going to be tough, but there was much planning to do. I knew that Bill would buy into the idea in no time, and he did, contributing to the efforts in invaluable ways. Throughout the coming year, I worked hard researching as many of the facts on Bill's birth, flight to the jungle and ultimate capture by the Japanese as I could. I made plans with a travel agent to retrace those steps—many steps that Bill had no knowledge of—and then made a small booklet of what I had already written for everyone to read on the plane.

Our first stop was Honolulu. There, on December 28th, we celebrated Bill's 76th birthday. We visited Pearl Harbor and were awed by the USS Arizona Memorial, a shrine that marks the resting place of 1,102 of the 1,177 sailors and Marines killed that fateful day of December 7, 1941. A visit to the USS Missouri, the Mighty Moe, where the unconditional surrender of the Japanese took place in Tokyo Bay, ending World War II, was equally sobering.

On December 30th, we boarded our plane to Manila and arrived early in the evening New Year's Eve. Our lodging, the beautiful Manila Hotel, was the very one Norwood and Isabel enjoyed upon their arrival in 1934. It was also General MacArthur's domicile while he served as military advisor to President Manuel Quezon before the war.

Happy New Year, 2017. Since everything in Manila was closed on New Year's Day, the travel agent had arranged a trip south to Tagaytay to climb the Taal volcano. It was not on our list of desired sites to visit and a tourist trap to boot. The novelty of the volcano is its small island in a lake inside the crater with the volcano itself on an island in a lake which is on an island in the Pacific. Tourist trap or no, it ended up being a fun day.   Next on our official itinerary: the island of Corregidor.

Boarding a ferry for a turbulent ride to "The Rock," we landed on the leeward side of the island due to the rough waters of the China Sea that lead into Manila Bay. Trams, much like trackless San Francisco trollies greeted us for our tour, and as luck would have it the guide on our tram was our very own Manila host Carlos. He made the island history come alive for us. Gun battery emplacements with twelve-inch mortars built in the early 1900's dot the island with six disappearing batteries that mechanically drop below ground level to avoid detection. The devastation of the military barracks that had housed the U.S. Regular Army, and other anti-aircraft detachments was extensive, and they stand as a testament to the many lost lives. A particular treat was a light show in the impressive Malinta tunnel that had protected and hospitalized our troops during the war.

As the day wore on the weather deteriorated, so much so that we were unable to sail back to Manila. The one small hotel boasting 30 rooms had 25 already booked, and there were probably 125-150 tourists stranded. Carlos incredibly secured a small room with two twin beds and a twin mattress on the floor—for five of us! Will chose the floor while the rest of us pushed the two twin beds together and squeezed in. Sleep, however, was elusive as a typhoon whipped the island all night long. A four a.m. wake-up call sent us back to the dock for the return trip to Manila, and although valuable time for our Manilan discoveries was lost, the adventure was a memory we would treasure forever. Right away our next site to visit was the principal reason for our trip: Santo Tomás University.

Upon seeing the long, low, grey granite marker of the university, tears filled our eyes. Bill had previously visited this hallowed ground while stationed at Clark AFB during the Viet Nam war, but for the rest of us, it was a new and emotional moment. Seeing the physical place where he and his family spent almost two of their three years as internees was riveting.

Awkwardly, Carlos had told us on the way that the university was closed for the holidays, and we would only be able to walk around outside. What? Had this family really traveled over 6,638 miles to walk around outside? We were stunned and frustrated beyond words. But Carlos, in Tagalog, the native tongue, convinced the guard at the Main Building's entrance to let us inside.

Unable to peer into the closed rooms to conceptualize how horribly crowded they must have been with 50-80 people living there, and not being allowed into the university museum which contained all the pictorial history of the internment was a terrible disappointment. But we *were* able to climb the main staircase where MacArthur had stopped for his visit after liberation and peer into the courtyards where many shanties had once stood. And all was not lost as Carlos knew an American internee in Manila who was a curator of the museum. A call to her helped somewhat to assuage our displeasure when she assured us that many of the pictures in the museum were the same ones we saw on Corregidor. And so, alas, it was time to move along.

Carlos was a bit uneasy when we asked him to take us to the North Cemetery. After explaining that we were searching for the grave of Jonathan's great-grandfather, he complied—uncomfortably. At the entrance gate, the keeper told Carlos that all records for American burials had been destroyed, but he would guide us to several areas that were possible sites. Driving in, we understood Carlos' disquiet. The place was an abomination. Indigents were camped among the graves with filth and refuse in every direction. Gravestones were toppled, and columbaria destroyed. Wary suspicious eyes watched our every move. We knew the grave was there because Jonathan's great-aunt had taken a picture years ago, but we had no idea in which sector to explore. We finally accepted reality, a second disappointment and gave up our search. It was now time to fly to Iloilo City on Panay Island, where much of the Carrolls' story began.

Seeing Iloilo, now a modern port city of over 440,000 people, was new for Bill. Unfortunately it was *after* our visit that I learned of Isabel and Norwood's address. It would have been amazing to see if their house was still standing, but our first order of business was to drive to Janiuay, the town of Bill's birth. Our young guide L.A. was also born in Janiuay, so he and Bill had an instant bond. It was sobering to stand under the huge arched city-center sign and imagine Isabel laboring through the night above a small schoolhouse, fearing what horrors lay ahead for her family and its newest tiny member as they fled from the Japanese. After taking pictures at the arch, L.A. gathered us for our next step of discovery: Cunsad.

Cunsad was where A.V.H. Hartendorp wrote that fifteen people, including the Carrolls, journeyed to hide from the Japanese. Norwood also made reference to it in May 1945 in the Durham Herald:

...with all the supplies that "we could beg, borrow, or steal we trekked inland to the hills of Cunsad, deep in the Panay jungles."

To get there, we had to take a jeepney—a converted, elongated army jeep that could contend with the rocky dirt road. The driver, with his wife and baby up front, expertly negotiated the rough thoroughfare, which again stirred our imagination of the Carrolls' intrepid march with a tiny baby Bill. Several people came out to greet us as we were the first American visitors to this tiny barangay in 76 years. Sharing coconuts and bananas, we communicated our appreciation through our guide—the area so remote that English was not spoken. One woman recounted that her 80-year-old mother remembered American families being captured by the Japanese. Chills enveloped us as we realized we were surely in the right place. It was hard to believe that we had found it.

A curiosity of this miniscule Filipino village as well as nearly every place we visited was a full-sized basketball court. The Filipinos idolize basketball, as does our North Carolina Tar Heel family. There was a court at the Taal volcano, Janiuay and now Cunsad. Earlier in our trip when the bell-hop at the Manila hotel saw Bill's UNC baseball cap, he asked if Bill played roundball for the team and rattled off every major player that ever wore a Carolina jersey. He then went on to name his NBA favorites. So when Bill, Will and Jonathan were offered a basketball in Cunsad, they enthusiastically scored a few hoops on our jungle visit.

Our bumpy ride back to Janiuay was contemplative as we reflected on our good fortune in finding Cunsad. Bill asked L.A. if, before returning to the hotel in Iloilo, we could stop at a place he spotted on the trip up to the jungle. He did not tell us what he saw, so we were surprised to drive into the Iloilo Golf Club—Norwood's playground. Strolling around the area we came to a museum-like building that housed all the silver trophies and paraphernalia that were saved before the Japanese burned the golf club down. In one glass case filled with memorabilia I saw a small silver monthly-trophy that stopped me in my tracks. I called everyone over to see if the little award looked familiar, hinting that a similar one sat in our living room at home. No one recognized it except Bill. Norwood won the exact same prize in December 1941—the date engraved on the side of the bowl—which meant that he had to have won the trophy right before Iloilo was bombed on December 18th. It was yet another thing that Norwood's servant had guarded and returned to him after the war. Seeing the trophy was serendipity at work once again.

The following morning began a tour that was to retrace the journey backwards from Iloilo to where the Japanese "bivouacked" the Carrolls after finding them in the jungle. Our first stop—which was the final one for the prisoners—was a visit to the corner of General Luna and Mabini Streets in search of the family's internment site. I fully expected to see an empty lot or perhaps a grocery store. But there on that corner, standing tall and newly restored was the Iloilo Elementary School where Bill and his family spent their first year under Japanese control. It was gripping to see Bill standing on the soil where he first crawled and then learned to walk 76 years ago.

Then across the Forbes bridge we drove, visualizing, as described earlier by Hartendorp, the trek over its partially bombed span that all fifteen of the newly captured prisoners had made when their train reached Iloilo. Our next stop: Pototan.

Pototan was the second place the Carrolls were taken after their capture. It was in that small town that the kind Magbanua family took in all fifteen prisoners, fed and gave shelter to them for the night. A street there named after Teresa Magbanua, a famous Filipina revolutionary, was where we asked our new guide Erma to stop and take a picture. As we continued our journey up from Iloilo, Erma

282

asked if we would like to meet the mayor of Pototan. Her friend worked for him and had secured a visitation. Although it was a kind offer we didn't particularly desire, we could hardly refuse. Upon arrival we went directly to the city's municipal building and after a short wait were ushered into the mayor's office. The Honorable Thomas M. Peñaflorida, sitting at his desk under a picture of President Rodrigo Duterte on the wall behind him, greeted us warmly. Cordial conversation led us to discover that the middle initial "M" in his name was his mother's maiden name— Magbanua! Did Erma know this when she arranged our visit? Was it possible the mayor's mother or perhaps an aunt was the woman who helped the beleaguered prisoners? Bill was deeply touched and thanked the mayor profusely for taking the time to meet with us. Buoyed by the extraordinary coincidence, we made our way to our next destination: Passi City.

After capture by the Japanese and the long arduous trek out of the jungle, especially difficult for Norwood with a painful tropical ulcer on his leg, the prisoners were taken to a convent in Passi City where they spent five anxious nights. This was the prisoners' first respite and our last stop on our journey to retrace Bill's footsteps through the Philippines. After taking pictures of the Parish of St.

283

Williams where they stayed, we headed for our journey's end: the island of Boracay.

At a beautiful retreat, we were able to reflect on the emotional and sometimes surreal discoveries we had experienced—the discoveries far outweighing the few disappointments. It was a perfect ending to a nearly perfect trip. Bill was awed, humbled and appreciative, and our children were grateful to finally see the foundation of their father's early life.

In the end, the question is what lasting impact did living in this parallel universe under Japanese oppression have on Bill and his family? Fortunately Bill and his siblings were young enough to have few or no memories of the hardships or horrors there. Nor did their basic health suffer from the privations. Norwood, though, was not so fortunate. His drastic weight loss affected his recovery, and he never quite regained his former vigor. He died at age 66 in 1973. Isabel lived a good long life in Durham and spent her last years in Asheboro near Peggy before her death at age 82 in 1989. At this writing Lee and Bill are still living. Peggy succumbed to her illness at age 77 in 2017.

While the little boy born in that far away land has no memory of the first three years of his life, the gratitude he feels for his parents is profound. His reverence for the fortitude those two people possessed is evident to all who know him. It marks Bill—it is who he is. For him and his family, especially our children, blessed be Norwood and Isabel Carroll. And for *everyone* who survived the cruelty of the Japanese, blessed be the brilliant, controversial and resolute General Douglas MacArthur whose command of countless brave soldiers brought about their liberation.

USS Arizona Memorial at Pearl Harbor

The Mighty Moe

The Manila Hotel

Off to the Taal Volcano

Bill on his strong kabayo heading up the volcano

Tiny island in a lake inside the volcano which is on an island in a lake which is on an island in the Pacific!

Standing at the edge of the caldera with Carlos our guide

Gun batteries on Corregidor

Military barracks before the war and now

Memorial on Corregidor

Bill with General MacArthur on Corregidor

The entrance to Santo Tomás University in Manila

Shanties during the war and a current view of the courtyard

The Main Building staircase where MacArthur visited

SANTO TOMAS INTERNMENT CAMP

THROUGH THESE PORTALS PASSED UP
TO TEN THOUSAND AMERICANS AND
OTHER NATIONALS OF THE FREE WORLD
WHO WERE INTERNED WITHIN THESE
WALLS BY THE JAPANESE MILITARY,
SUFFERING GREAT PHYSICAL PRIVATION
AND NATIONAL HUMILIATION FROM JAN-
UARY 4, 1942 UNTIL LIBERATED FEBRUY
3, 1945, BY THE AMERICAN FORCES
UNDER GENERAL DOUGLAS MacARTHUR.

FEBRUARY 1954   AMERICAN ASSOCIATION
                     OF THE PHILIPPINES

Scenes from the North Cemetery

Bill at Janiuay, the town of his birth

A WWII jeep elongated into a jeepney used for public transport

Heading to Cunsad

The kind people of Cunsad. The woman on the far left said her 80 year-old mother remembered American families being captured by the Japanese!

Basketball at Cunsad

A Filipino riding his carabao

Norwood's Golf Club

Monthly medal at Iloilo Golf Club and
Norwood's medal dated December 1941

Bill at Iloilo Elementary School where he spent one year as an prisoner of the Japanese: from age 6 months to 1 ½ years old

Bill with the mayor of Pototan

A street named after Teresa Magbanua, the Filipina
revolutionary whose relative aided the Carrolls and the other
prisoners on their way to Iloilo Internment Camp

Fields of roosters on the way to Passi City.
Cockfighting is a Filipino passion

Parish of St. Williams today where the Carrolls spent the first
five nights after capture by the Japanese

Our beautiful resort on Borocay with a sunset view
looking toward home

Afterword

Researching and recording the story of Bill's birth and early years became an all-consuming fascination for me. I stumbled upon so many missing pieces, several of which were a surprise for Bill. Finding the book by A.V.H. Hartendorp, cited many times, was the greatest windfall in my search. Suddenly there was a portrait of the Carrolls' entire flight to the jungle and subsequent capture. It was almost as if a Google Map landed in my lap.

Many of the diaries of STIC internees were more than illuminating. Their words painted pictures that were sometimes wrenching and oftentimes humorous. But the greatest reveal was the strength and will they possessed in believing that freedom would surely come. The vast majority refused to give up hope.

Reading the many books about the cruelty of the Japanese, however, was difficult. More people died in Japanese POW camps than in all of the POW camps in Europe. Their brutality was inflicted on more than 140,000 Allied prisoners who were starved to skeletons and worked to death as slaves if they weren't first hacked apart, cannibalized, burned alive, or dissected alive as guinea pigs for experiments in germ warfare and medical sadism.

The death rate in Japanese POW camps was 27% compared to a 4% death rate in German camps. In clear violation of the Geneva Convention, the treatment of American and Allied prisoners was one of the abiding horrors of World War II. Although STIC was not by strict definition an American and Allied POW camp, the civilians there experienced intense suffering their last year . The death rate there was nearly 10%.

Why were the Japanese so cruel? What made them behave with such savagery? A book by Gavan Daws, *Prisoners of the Japanese: POWs of World War II in the Pacific,* shed some light on that question for me. He writes that during the Russo-Japanese War at the beginning of the century, the Japanese committed no comparable atrocities against prisoners. In fact they were actually commended by the International Red Cross for their humane treatment of their captives. The Japanese military caste was far smaller and governed by a purer Samurai cultural tradition. But during World War II, the military was vastly expanded which resulted in a general coarsening of the officer status. Crude peasants, and unprincipled young men corrupted the honorable Japanese warrior tradition. According to Daws:

A kind of madness came over the nation. You had hundreds of thousands of people who had never exercised authority at home and suddenly had unlimited power over captive populations. And since commanding or guarding a prison camp was considered a less than honorable assignment by the Japanese, the chances of getting an honorable Japanese handling Allied POWs, one who cared about justice and wouldn't countenance horrors in Japan's name, was pretty small.

The official policy for years in Japan was to sanitize World War II, and as a result much of the population is not aware of what really happened. Many young Japanese believe that Japan declared war on the United States before launching the attack at Pearl Harbor. The fact that the rest of the world has indisputable evidence to the contrary is irrelevant. From Daws:

A small but slowly growing number of Japanese historians have been fighting the systematic suppression of history in recent years, insisting the country come honestly to terms with its treatment of captive nations during the war. They are ostracized, they get death threats, but they don't give up.

An article in the Chicago Tribune reported that in 1944, when Japan was nearing defeat, Tokyo's military planners came up with an astonishing plan to strike back at America. Huge balloons were launched that rode the prevailing winds to the continental United States. Although the American government censored reports at the time, some

311

200 balloons landed in Western states, and bombs carried by the balloons killed a woman in Montana and six people in Oregon Again from Daws:

> The treatment of Allied prisoner of war, like Japan's other atrocities of World War II, is something Japan inevitably must see requires sincere acknowledgment and apologies. Until it does, no one, not even the Japanese can be certain it won't happen again.

Angus Lorenzen, a STIC internee, expresses the issue in his book *A Lovely Little War:*

> For young people, my message is to not be ashamed or apologetic for what happened during the war. That happened many years ago and was the responsibility of people two, three, or more generations ahead of you. The world is a very different place today, and we all hope that the horror can never happen again, and that the young people will lead the way of ensuring that it does not.
>
> For the older people, and particularly the politicians, I want to say that they must stop denying Japan's culpability for creating a holocaust in East Asia. It is time to apologize to all those people who are now fading away that bore the brunt by disease, torture, and death of Japan's Imperial ambitions. Tell the truth—don't propagandize what you did!

No nation or race holds a monopoly on virtue, this is sure. War makes just people do grossly unjust things. But Japan's depravity sank to levels beyond comprehension.

For those, like Bill, who are still living long after the misery of their oppression, it is important to make known what they endured. Not only did they have to learn to live without the freedom they knew before capture, but they also had to grapple with simply trying to survive a cruel regime of starvation. The citizens of Manila faced different privations during the occupation, but no one could foresee or even imagine the shocking and savage murders visited upon them as the American soldiers drew near. Little of their merciless deaths are in our history books, and the battles to free the Philippines are given scant recognition. Additionally, there are precious few memorials to Allied soldiers who died in Asian camps, let alone tributes to the brutalized survivors who had to make peace with their freedom after the war.

Through this narrative, it is my hope that some of the truths are revealed. And it is with this account that I honor my husband, his family and all the brave souls of Santo Tomás Internment Camp and Manila.

Bill's camp ID card

His certificate of citizenship secured in 1966

314

SURGERY
E. C. FOSTER, M. D., F. A. C. S.   CONSULTANT
JOHN A. HATCH, M. D.
GLENN C. HATCH, M. D., F. A. C. S.
HENRY S. WATERS, M. D., F. A. C. S.
DUNDEE, N. Y.

MEDICINE
ALLEN W. HOLMES, M. D.
ROBERT F. LEWIS, M. D.
JOHN L. SAULTS, M. D.

DONALD M. TREADWELL, M. D.
DUNDEE, N. Y.

FOSTER-HATCH MEDICAL GROUP

100 MAIN ST.
PENN YAN, N. Y.

50 WATER ST.
DUNDEE, N. Y.

This is to certify that I am a citizen of the United States, a resident of Dundee, N. Y., a physician registered in Yates County, State of New York, and that I practiced medicine in Iloilo City, Philippines, from 1934 to 1948.

Further, that on December 28, 1941, I attended the birth of William Singleton Carroll, in Iloilo City, Philippines, born to Mr. and Mrs. Marcbel A. Carroll.

Henry S. Waters, M. D.

Jan 26, 1950   Henry S. Waters, M. D.

STATE OF NEW YORK)
COUNTY OF YATES) ss.:

On this 27th day of January, 1950, before me, the subscriber, personally appeared Henry S. Waters, M.D., to me personally known and known to me to be the same person described in and who executed the within Instrument, and he duly acknowledged to me that he executed the same.

HAROLD J. STEELE
NOTARY PUBLIC

Documentation of Bill's birth by Dr. Henry Waters who attended his birth during the Carrolls' flight to the jungle.

315

Bill in Saigon during the Vietnam War

Acknowledgements

I give thanks to my good friend Kathryn Thompson for her expert guidance in editing this book. The time spent absorbing and correcting the manuscript went beyond expectations—for her and for me. Kathryn's suggestions for clarity and change were professional, thoughtful and direct, and most of them I followed.

I also wish to thank my husband Bill for his patience in awaiting the final result. It was important for me to get it right.

Bibliography

Cates, Tressa R. *The Drainpipe Diary, My Internment at Santo Tomás.* New York, NY: Vantage Press 1957

Gowen, Vincent H. *Sunrise to Sunrise: One Man's Journey through History: China, The Philippines and World War II Internment.* Victoria, Canada: Traffor Publishing, 2008.

Hartendorp, A.V.H. *The Japanese Occupation of the Philippines Volume I.* Manila: Bookmark, 1967.

Holland, Robert B. *100 Miles to Freedom: The Epic Story of the Rescue of Santo Tomás and the Liberation of Manila: 1943-1945.* Nashville, TN: Turner Publishing Company, 2011.

Johansenn, Bruce E. *So Far From Home: Manila's Santo Tomás Internment Camp 1942-1945.* Omaha, NE: PBI Press, 1967.

Manchester, William. *American Caesar: Douglas MacArthur 1880-1964.* New York, NY: Little, Brown and Company, 1976.

Vaughn, Elizabeth (edited by Carol M. Petillo). *The Ordeal of Elizabeth Vaughan: A Wartime Diary of the Philippines.* Athens, GA: The University of Georgia Press, 1985.

Scott, James M. *Rampage: MacArthur, Yamashita, and the Battle of Manila.* New York, NY: W.W. Norton & Company, Inc. 2018

Van Sickle, Emily. *The Iron Gates of Santo Tomás: The Firsthand Account of an American Couple Interned by the Japnese in Manila, 1942-1945.* Chicago, IL: Academy Chicago Publishers, 1992.

Wygle, Peter. *Surviving a Japanese P.O.W. Camp: Father and Son Endure Internment in Manila During World War II.* Ventura, CA: Pathfinder Publising of CA, 1991

319

About The Author

McLean (Lean) Goodpasture Carroll, a native of
Bristol, Virginia is a graduate of Hollins University in
Roanoke, Virginia. She received a Bachelor of Arts
degree in Music and currently maintains an active piano
teaching studio that she has enjoyed for the last 40 years.

Lean lives with her husband Bill in Bellevue,
Washington where together they raised two children, a son
Will and a daughter Tilghman.

Made in the USA
Middletown, DE
22 March 2019